# *Redemptive* DIVORCE

A Biblical Process that Offers Guidance for the
Suffering Partner, Healing for the Offending Spouse,
and the Best Catalyst for Restoration

**Mark W. Gaither**

**THOMAS NELSON**
*Since 1798*

NASHVILLE   DALLAS   MEXICO CITY   RIO DE JANEIRO   BEIJING

Published in Nashville, Tennessee, by Thomas Nelson. Thomas Nelson is a registered trademark of Thomas Nelson, Inc.

Published in association with the literary agency of WordServe Literary Group, Ltd., 10152 S. Knoll Circle, Highlands Ranch, Colorado 80130.

Thomas Nelson, Inc. titles may be purchased in bulk for educational, business, fund-raising, or sales promotional use. For information, please e-mail SpecialMarkets@ThomasNelson.com.

This publication is intended to provide authoritative information in regard to the subject matter covered. It is purchased with the understanding that divorce laws may vary from state to state and that the publisher is not giving advice nor rendering legal, accounting, or other professional services. If you require legal advice or other expert assistance, you should seek the services of a competent professional in that field.

Unless otherwise noted, Scripture quotations are taken from the New American Standard Bible,® © The Lockman Foundation 1960, 1962, 1963, 1968, 1971, 1972, 1973, 1975, 1977, 1995. Used by permission.

Scripture quotations marked NET are from The NET Bible, New English Translation. © 1996–2007 by Biblical Studies Press, L.L.C., www.bible.org. All rights reserved.

Scripture quotations marked NIV are from the Holy Bible: New International Version.® © 1973, 1978, 1984 by International Bible Society. Used by permission of Zondervan Publishing House. All rights reserved.

**Library of Congress Cataloging-in-Publication Data**

Gaither, Mark W., 1962–
    Redemptive divorce : a biblical process that offers guidance for the suffering partner, healing for the offending spouse, and the best catalyst for restoration / Mark W. Gaither.
      p. cm.
    ISBN 978-0-7852-2856-1 (pbk.)
    1. Divorce—Religious aspects—Christianity. I. Title.
BT707.G35 2008
248.8'46—dc22                                          2008005526

*Printed in the United States of America*

08 09 10 11 12 RRD 5 4 3 2 1

# Praise for
## Redemptive Divorce

"Thank God for the courage of Mark Gaither. Out of the crucible of his own experience and the grid of Scripture, Mark provides practical direction and encouragement for Christians whose marriages are broken or unbearable. The good news: you don't have to remain passive or suffer in silence anymore. Divorce is an ugly word, but *Redemptive Divorce* is an assertive plan that enables you to use the courts and the law while still being genuinely Christian."

— DAVE CARDER
Pastor, Counseling Ministries,
First Evangelical Free Church,
Fullerton, CA; Author, *Torn Asunder* and *Close Calls*

"Finally, we have some fresh, creative, and practical thinking on an issue that has divided many believers. I appreciate the emphasis that has been given to the individual who is creating the problem rather than putting so much ill-placed responsibility upon the victim. This resource is bound to create some healthy discussion and, hopefully, some changes and perspective within the church."

— H. NORMAN WRIGHT
Author, Professor, and Grief
Trauma Therapist

"I've never read a more sensitive, biblically balanced and carefully researched book than *Redemptive Divorce*. It will be a source of clarity and inspiration to anyone struggling with the question, 'How can a Christian divorce?' Mark is to be commended; his book is simply brilliant. I only wish it had been written decades ago."

— Marilyn Meberg
Women of Faith® Speaker;
Author, *Love Me, Never Leave Me*

*For Charissa,*

*my daily reminder of God's greatest gift,*

*His grace.*

# Contents

contents

# Foreword

Several years ago, my wife and I were on a large ship leaving the New York harbor. It was a beautiful late-summer evening. The lights of Manhattan were behind us, the open sea was ahead of us, and the highly elevated Varrazano Narrows Bridge would soon be above us. Our fellow passengers were standing on the main deck all around us, snapping pictures as they did their best to take it all in.

My focus was on our nation's best-known monument, the beloved Statue of Liberty. I stared in silence at her stately presence. The proud lady is dressed in a loose robe that falls in graceful folds to the top of the pedestal on which she stands. Her left arm grasps a tablet on which is etched the date of our Declaration of Independence. Her right arm extends high into the sky; her hand holds a torch. At her feet is a broken shackle representing the overthrow of tyranny.

As my eyes drifted across Ellis Island, I paused and imagined scenes of yesteryear, where boatloads of bewildered, frightened, and lonely immigrants once stood, going through a confusing process, trying to understand the questions, struggling with a language not their own, all the while reaching down to comfort their tearful and fearful children. There they were, thousands of miles from everything that had been familiar to them, finding refuge under the shadow of a hundred tons of compassion from that strong lady who stood tall and stately in their defense, a mute testimony to the message inscribed on the bronze plaque beneath her robe—a sonnet of touching words by Emma Lazarus, ending with:

> Give me your tired, your poor,
> Your huddled masses yearning to breathe free,
> The wretched refuse of your teeming shore.
> Send these, the homeless, the tempest-tossed to me:
> I lift my lamp beside the golden door.

I remembered that meaningful moment in the New York harbor when I read Mark Gaither's volume—the book you hold in your hands. I paused and imagined those who would find refuge in these carefully written pages. I identified especially with you who are where I have never been: facing your own bewildering, frightening, and lonely future apart from everything that has been familiar to you. To borrow from Mark's own words, you are "the weary guardians of . . . dead or dying unions [who] can do very little" on your own.

Put simply, you need an *advocate*. You need someone who truly understands what you are enduring, who can help you through the process, who is willing to walk beside you, and who will help you get underway before your pain screams louder than the voice of reason.

Mark Gaither is qualified to be that advocate. He understands. Because he was, himself, once there, he has long since left the ivory towers of idealism; his is a real world. Because he is, himself, a keen student of the Bible with a firm grip on sound theology, he will not lead you astray. His counsel is reliable, fair, and balanced. That means you don't have to worry that he is going to twist the Scriptures to fit some extreme ideas he's originated or that you buy into a pile of weird theories he's promoting. For the sake of you who do not know him, let me verify that Mark Gaither is a man whose life is marked by theological veracity and personal integrity.

As Mark has stated, he wrote *Redemptive Divorce* "to help people drowning in the chaos of dysfunction and held down by a theological conundrum." Rather than dodging the practical issues and performing semantic footwork when faced with the teachings of God's Word, Mark answers the hard questions. Rather than merely quoting Bible verses and using pious clichés when dealing with longstanding offenses that break the heart and wound the soul of a marriage, he acknowledges the difficulties of navigating through the minefields of uncertainty, disharmony, anger, and even danger. Throughout the process of writing his book, Mark has remembered that this is counsel for not only those going through the pain of a fractured relationship but also you who love those in that struggle and who desperately wish to help them.

Think of yourself as someone who is tired and bewildered, having endured a tempest-tossed journey. Think of Mark Gaither as a calm and responsible advocate who has a heart for all who yearn to breathe free, who stands tall and strong in a harbor of refuge, welcoming you in, offering you truth to live by and a reason to go on. Think of this volume as a lamp, holding high a torch of understanding and compassion. And then, think of your future as a new and different journey where forgiveness and grace replace rage and revenge and where hope and healing displace loneliness and despair.

—CHARLES R. SWINDOLL
Founding and Senior Pastor,
Stonebriar Community Church
Bible Teacher, *Insight for Living*
Chancellor, Dallas Theological
Seminary
Father-in-law of Mark Gaither

# Acknowledgments

I owe a great debt to Mary Graham, Luci Swindoll, and Tami Heim for their encouragement when I first shared my idea for this book, and especially to Tami for wholeheartedly supporting my proposal to Thomas Nelson. Without their sincere affirmation, I don't know that I would have found the courage to pursue this project. And endless thanks to my beautiful bride, Charissa, for insisting that I put my fingers to the keyboard and get this resource into print.

Many thanks to Steve Fischer, pastor of biblical counseling at Stonebriar Community Church, for allowing me access to his wealth of knowledge and experience gained from many years in Christian counseling. Our discussions not only kept my creative fire burning when doubt threatened to put it out, but they frequently turned a jumble of thoughts into something meaningful.

As the manuscript neared completion, the insightful critique of two men kept my focus clear: Kim Cheatum, with nearly thirty years in family law, and Dave Carder, whose work with couples recovering from infidelity is nothing less than pioneering. Each of their perspectives has been shaped by many years in the trenches, and they helped me keep everything real.

Finally, mere words will never adequately express the deep gratitude

I have for Chuck Swindoll and what he has meant to me spiritually, vocationally, and personally. Words like *authenticity* and *integrity* became key terms in my vocabulary as I listened to his sermons on the radio and read his books. Then, his tutelage honed a crude capacity for writing into something sharp enough to prepare this volume. But nothing will come close to the great privilege of seeing the man for all he is—"warts and everything"—yet finding nothing surprising, except perhaps a deeper desire to be like Christ than he reveals in the pulpit.

# Introduction

I never imagined I would write a book with the word *divorce* in the title, and certainly not from personal experience. But one summer evening just after my third year in seminary, a whirlwind of infidelity lifted my household off its foundation and landed us in a place I never expected to see firsthand. In a span of about eight hours, I was transformed from a happily married family man to a suddenly single father of two.

For a little more than two weeks, I made just about every mistake you can make in a situation like mine. I begged, I wooed, I bargained, I preached, I prophesied doom, and I kept it a secret from all but a select few. Then I began to worry about how this might affect my two young teens, so I asked the seminary for the name of a Christian family law attorney.

The day before my first appointment, a friend recommended I read Dr. James Dobson's *Love Must Be Tough*. I found a copy at a second-hand bookstore, took it home, and devoured it in one night. The following afternoon, I sat across from an attorney in a modest office, surrounded by stacks of legal documents.

"What's your first priority?" he asked.

"First, I want to make sure the kids stay with me," I answered.

"And then?"

"I want to save my marriage."

"Good," he said with a sharp nod. "Then I'll take your case."

For the remainder of the hour, he explained his unorthodox philosophy concerning divorce. He advocated what today might be termed a "shock and awe" approach to cases like mine. He typically prepared as aggressive a petition and decree as the courts would allow, hoping the legal jolt would shake some sense into the wayward partner. I asked if he had read Dobson's book about tough love. He hadn't.

I doubted that the intersection of my tragedy, Dobson's book, and this particular attorney was mere coincidence. I had earnestly prayed that God would somehow turn this disaster into something good. Of course, my prayer was aimed at my broken family. God's sights were a bit higher. I pursued redemption through to its conclusion with no regrets, and in the years since then, I have researched and refined what I now call *redemptive divorce*.

Shortly before I began writing this book, I encountered a woman who had endured years of emotional and verbal abuse from her husband and whose children had been reduced to bundles of raw nerves. Her husband maintained a Christian public facade that made Billy Graham look like a barbarian, but he became something quite different behind closed doors. When his sarcasm wasn't shredding anyone nearby, the walls of their home literally resonated with his rage.

I desperately tried to walk her through the redemptive divorce process, but she no longer had ears to hear anything but the word *escape*, which she spelled D-I-V-O-R-C-E. She didn't have the energy or even the desire to pursue reconciliation anymore. And, frankly, I didn't blame her. Redemption requires strength, and she had none left. She spent it all surviving and trying to keep her children from self-destructing. Unfortunately, her friends and her church did little more than add to her burden by insisting that she trust the Lord and remain faithful to her wedding day promises—something she had already done to the point of despair.

That's when I realized that the audience for this book needed to include pastors, counselors, attorneys, family members, and friends of those struggling to survive dysfunctional marriages. The weary guardians of these dead or dying unions can do very little on their own. They need advocates, people who understand this process and who are willing to walk beside them on their journey. Moreover, these hurting spouses need to get this process underway before their pain screams louder than the voice of reason.

Each time I described this project, the conversation rarely ended without one or more people noting that someone they knew needed this book. Pastors and counselors eagerly requested advance copies of the manuscript because the need for this tool could not wait. Each had several clients and parishioners who desperately needed solutions the church did not provide. And I saw something in the eyes of those who understand the complexities of trying to help someone trapped in a dysfunctional marriage. It was a mixture of hope and *eureka!* Perhaps it's the same expression that crossed Alexander Fleming's face when he realized that penicillin could kill bacteria. Through the process of redemptive divorce, they could finally offer genuine hope to these hurting spouses without ignoring the authority of Scripture or pretending that marriage isn't supposed to be permanent.

I wrote *Redemptive Divorce* to help people drowning in the chaos of dysfunction and held down by a theological conundrum. What should they do when their mate becomes impossible, even dangerous to live with? How can they stay afloat when the commands of Christ to love and forgive feel like a millstone? I wrote it *for* these people, but I wrote it *to* those who want to help them. Therefore, the first four chapters lay a solid biblical and theological foundation for the last four chapters, which describe the process of redemptive divorce in practical terms. By the end, I hope a great need will have been met in the lives of suffering people and in the church, which desperately wants to help them. The redemptive divorce process offers practical relief for the suffering partner and healing hope to the offending spouse. And, in some cases, it might even be the catalyst for the restoration and rebuilding of the marriage.

May the Lord bless you, keep you, inspire you, and empower you as you read.

# One

## Suffering or Divorce? Finding a Way Out of the No-Win Scenario

"I don't believe in divorce." As Diane responded to the pleas of her non-Christian friends, the waver in her voice dignified her desperate resolve. Some might have even called her convictions heroic. Her husband of sixteen years, however, had demonstrated all too clearly by his love of alcohol and rage that he did not share her perspective on marriage. The sacred covenant she entered as a young woman had become his license to drink and hurl insults with no consequences. And after a thousand broken promises and countless wasted hours in counseling, Diane was at the breaking point. For the sake of her children's safety and sanity, and for the survival of her own withered soul, something had to change. Unfortunately, her family, her church, and her own Christian conscience spoke in heartbroken, anguished accord: "I don't believe in divorce."

Diane's resolute trust in God's goodness had sustained her in the midst of her trials, but the hopelessness of her situation became clearer after two conversations: one with her friend, Marge, and the other with her pastor, Ron.

## Stand Up and Get Out!

Diane quietly ate her lunch as Marge picked at her salad. After a long silence, Marge looked up and said, "I haven't been to Sunday school since I was a child, so I don't know much about God. But I don't see how a marriage like yours is something He would find very pleasing."

Marge had been married to her high school sweetheart for more than twenty years and enjoyed the kind of relationship that Diane had long since given up hope of having. "Do you think it's God's will for you to live this way?" She rested her elbows on the cafeteria table and stared intently into Diane's eyes.

"No," Diane replied patiently. "God isn't pleased with a lot of things on earth, but that doesn't mean that I should answer Gary's sin by committing another sin, like getting a divorce."

"Sin?" Marge looked incredulous.

"Marge, I know you don't see marriage the way I do, but I believe that Gary and I entered a sacred, unbreakable covenant on our wedding day. The Bible says, 'God hates divorce.'"

Marge looked down, shook her head, and then put a sympathetic hand on Diane's. "Honey, Gary's in love with alcohol, and he's never cared for anyone but himself. He's already broken your covenant. Look, I don't pretend to know as much about the Bible as you, but I do know something about marriage. I completely believe in commitment. I said, 'For better and for worse,' and I meant it. But it seems to me that choosing to be Gary's doormat and allowing him to live however he wants only makes a mockery of what you hold sacred. Sounds like to me you're okay with him wiping his feet on you and your vows. You're treating your covenant as badly as he is."

Anger flashed like lightning in Diane's chest. She had never been accused of dishonoring her vows before. In fact, she had been universally praised for her steadfast commitment through the worst of circumstances—a rare and precious reward in an otherwise thankless life. "How am I guilty of dishonoring my covenant?" she snapped.

Marge sat back in her chair and let the moment pass in silence. Then she asked, "Does the Bible teach that you and Gary are equals in the marriage?"

"There's a lot of disagreement in churches, but I believe that Gary is supposed to be the leader and I should follow him. And if he *could* lead, I would *want* to follow him." Diane laughed. "That's probably the last thing a feminist would want to hear, especially from the wife of an alcoholic."

"No, but that's not what I mean. Does the Bible teach that you and Gary are equally *valuable*?"

"Well, of course!"

Marge leaned forward again. "Do you think God approves of how Gary treats you?"

"You know He doesn't."

"You must think He does. Because what I hear you saying is that the vows you made before God make it okay for Gary to hurt you without having to face any consequences. If God wants you to clean Gary's house, cook his meals, care for his children, and play the 'good wife' for the sake of his career, and if leaving him is a sin . . . well, it seems to me that God likes Gary a whole lot more than He likes you. At least that's how you're acting."

Echoes of Al-Anon meetings—months of them—reverberated in Diane's head. She felt confident that she had pushed past denial, but now . . . Had she merely sanctified her inability to defend her own dignity as a person?

"Diane, I love you," Marge said, "and I really do respect your beliefs. But your vows—at least the way you see them—have become a prison and you're letting a madman hold the keys. I just can't believe that God thinks as little of you as you think of yourself. I can't believe that refusing to accept Gary's destructive behavior is something God would consider a sin. Not if He loves you."

Diane wiped her tears with a napkin. "I know I'm worth more than how I'm treated, but I want to do everything I can to save my marriage. I just don't know what to do right now."

"I can understand that, but what about your kids?" Marge lowered her voice and said urgently, "What do you think this is teaching them? What kind of husband do you think Sean will become after watching his dad get by with this kind of behavior?"

Diane shuddered at the thought of her son becoming like his father.

"And what kind of husband are you encouraging Anne to choose? If not for the sake of your own dignity, then for the sake of your children, get those keys back and get out of that torture chamber you call a marriage!"

Tears rolled down Diane's cheeks as she tried to keep a sob from escaping. She couldn't deny the truth coming from her non-Christian friend. Certainly the Lord wanted something better for her, but she thought, *If marriage is "for better or for worse," isn't this "the worse"? If marriage is "in sickness or in health," isn't Gary's addiction a disease?*

## Don't Give Up!

Diane's instinct told her that Marge was wrong, but her friend had made some valid points, so she made an appointment to talk with her pastor, Ron. He was well aware of Gary's drinking, his verbal assaults, and the emotional war zone he had made of the household. Pastor Ron had been in regular contact with the couple for the better part of three years, meeting with them personally, arranging professional counseling, encouraging them, teaching them . . . everything a pastor could do, Ron had done to the point of exhaustion and exasperation.

He and the other leaders of the church stood by Diane countless times as she applied "tough love," refusing to help Gary when he was drunk, taking the children to a friend's when he became verbally abusive, even compelling him to attend counseling with her. But every breakthrough or turnaround proved to be nothing more than a clever con game. Eventually, Ron and the church leaders accepted that only a miracle would change Gary, so they shifted their focus to helping Diane cope.

Diane could plainly see that her situation broke Ron's heart. Empathy laced each word as he spoke. "I'll be honest with you, Diane; I don't understand God sometimes. And situations like yours take me back to the Scriptures again and again for reassurance that what I tell you is right. And every time, I come away with the same answer. Divorce is not an option in your particular situation. If it were up to me, I'd tell you to end the marriage, enjoy your freedom, and heal from this awful mess. But if you're asking me what the Bible teaches . . ." Ron shook his head and sighed.

Diane pleaded, "So the Bible says Gary can cheat on me with the bottle and destroy our family—as long as he doesn't sleep with someone else?" She desperately hoped to find a loophole in the contract that held her captive.

"Like I said, I don't understand why the Lord allows evil to continue. I just know that He loves you and that He is right in all His ways. And I cannot ignore what Jesus said."

Diane searched Ron's eyes and saw desperate authenticity staring back at her. As a man of the Book, he would not allow his personal feelings to invalidate the call of Scripture to obey. Diane slumped forward and said, "I don't know how much more I can take. I don't know if the damage already done to Sean and Anne can ever be undone. And it's only getting worse."

As Diane began to sob, Ron motioned for his assistant to come. She put her arm around Diane and squeezed her tightly as he pulled his chair closer and looked intently into Diane's eyes. "God has promised that He will not allow anything more than you can endure, which is not to say that your burden will be easy. We all have our crosses to bear, and this one is yours. Remain steadfast in your promises to Gary, and let the Lord honor your faithfulness in His time and in His way. And who knows? Your husband may be 'won without a word.' All things are possible with God, Diane. Don't give up. We're with you no matter what happens."

At that moment, Diane felt like something died within her. She wasn't quite sure what it was, and perhaps it needed to die. She felt some relief in the truth of Ron's words, but he clearly didn't understand the gravity of what he was asking her to do. And he would not likely approve of what she planned to do next.

## Christian Limbo

Diane found herself hopelessly trapped between two intolerable options: pursue a divorce without clear biblical support or continue to endure a life of unrelenting misery. Neither choice resonated within her as "right," yet neither embodied the values she had studied in Scripture most of her life. To make matters worse, conversations with her friends and family brought more confusion than clarity. Choosing to honor one godly principle inevitably put her at odds with another. It's a no-win scenario faced by thousands of conscientious followers of Jesus Christ who presently suffer in dysfunctional or dangerous marriages.

A person can endure this no-win scenario for months, even years, but not forever. As James Dobson so eloquently put it,

> The human mind cannot tolerate agitated depression and grief indefinitely. The healthy personality will act to protect itself in time, throwing off the despair and groping for stability. One method by which this is accomplished is by turning pain into anger.[1]

Given enough time, people in situations like Diane's reach a breaking point and often make destructive or unwise choices. And the intensity of their emotional backlash can be frightening, especially against the offending spouse and anyone who had encouraged them to "remain faithful to their vows." Feeling forsaken by friends, family, church, and even God Himself, some abandon themselves to an adulterous affair and desert their families, ironically giving their sinning spouse biblical grounds for divorce. Many others eventually decide that while God may not approve of their divorce, they cannot continue to exist in the moral limbo to which they have been relegated, and they choose what they consider to be the lesser of two evils: a divorce that their loved ones and church friends do not support.

To be perfectly fair, leaders in Christian ministry face the no-win scenario on a grand scale. For them, the implications extend far beyond the suffering of just one person and his or her family. Also at stake are the institution of marriage and the authority of Scripture.

## Protecting Marriage

For many decades, Christian pastors, teachers, counselors, and sociologists have lamented the steady, undeniable erosion of marriage and feel compelled to shore it up, even if it means that some individuals must suffer. As the divorce rate climbs, church leaders elevate the institution of marriage. The more the world profanes marriage, the more sacred it becomes in the minds of those who defend it. As more people freely discard the marriage covenant at will, the response has been to proclaim the inviolable, unbreakable nature of the one-flesh bond more fervently and more rigidly than before. This progression has escalated to the point that we now place such high value on marriage that we are willing to sacrifice almost anything to avoid divorce, including the safety and spiritual well-being of individuals. This may explain the disheartening results of a survey conducted by James and Phyllis Alsdurf. They questioned pastors to determine when they would support a battered woman's decision to separate from her abuser.

> One-third of the respondents felt that the abuse would have to be life-threatening. Almost one-fifth believed that no amount of abuse would justify a woman leaving, while one in seven felt a moderate expression of violence would be justification enough. The remainder interpreted "occasional" violence as grounds for leaving.
>
> However, only two percent of the pastors said they would support a divorce in situations of violence.[2]

We must ask ourselves, was man made for marriage or marriage made for man? Are we becoming guilty of venerating the institution of marriage over its original design, like the Pharisees obsessed over the Sabbath? (Mark 2:27) Have we lost sight of the purpose of marriage in God's ultimate program to make us more like Christ? As one minister's wife discovered, having no way to address her husband's cavalier attitude toward his sin inevitably gave Satan an opportunity to poison her heart.

*My husband is a pastor, and a little over a year ago, he had an affair with at least one woman. He may have sinned with other women, but I can't be sure. He only admits to what he's been caught at. Still, he constantly reminds me how I need to be obedient to God's word and how I should respect him no matter what he has done.* Yet all I can think is, Were you obedient to the Word of God when you were committing willful sin against me, your congregation, and your God? *He doesn't care about obeying God. He only uses the Bible and guilt to keep me in line and avoid talking about his own sin.*

*I know what the Bible says about divorce, and I don't want to divorce him even though I know I have the right to. But I'm not staying in the marriage because I love him. Frankly, I don't anymore. My children love their father, his congregation respects him, and everyone would be devastated if I exposed him for what he really is. He doesn't want a divorce but only because he doesn't want the expense and the embarrassment. Plus, he needs someone to keep his house and raise his children.*

*I don't like feeling this way. I hate the bitterness and resentment in my heart, but I can't get rid of these awful feelings. It makes me literally sick sometimes, and I feel like I'm not the person I once was. But I don't want to go through the rest of my life with this unforgiveness and anger. I'm afraid it will turn into hatred.*

*Sometimes I think getting divorced would be better. Staying married to him only keeps me from being the wife I should be, and I can't keep myself from the sin of resentment and bitterness. How can I possibly submit to him or respect him as a leader? Everything I read and all of my family and friends say that divorce is wrong. But why did God permit it in some situations?*

*I am so tired. I'm tired of being confused. I'm tired of trying to love someone who only loves himself. I'm tired of trying to be a good wife for a man who doesn't even know what one looks like. I don't know what to do. Please pray for me.*

*Linda*

While this pastor's wife struggles to remain faithful in her walk with Christ, her faithfulness to her vows (despite her husband's sin and arrogance) has become a spiritual liability. This should never be!

## Obeying God's Word

For Christian leaders, the debate over divorce also impacts the authority of Scripture. Jesus, when asked about divorce, stated that a husband and wife "are no longer two, but one flesh. What therefore God has joined together, let no man separate" (Matt. 19:6) and "Whoever divorces his wife, except for [sexual] immorality, and marries another woman commits adultery" (Matt. 19:9).[3] The interpretation of these words is a proving ground for how one will interpret and apply Scripture in general. And it's a particularly difficult issue because it seemingly places two of God's primary attributes, love and righteousness, in direct contention.

Many people correctly argue that God's love would not want to prolong Diane's domestic torture, but their arguments typically set aside His righteousness. And the arguments against taking the words of Jesus at face value are legion.

- "Jesus answered a specific question, so we can't apply His statement universally."
- "Jesus didn't mean what we think He did."
- "Cultures and contexts are no longer the same. That was then; this is now."

Some of the arguments are intriguing—even compelling at first blush—but they all accomplish the same result. They effectively render the words of Christ meaningless, which leaves many believers feeling uneasy. And rightfully so. Any solution to this moral dilemma must not ignore the words of Jesus or rob them of their meaning.

On the other hand, many Christians correctly take the words of Scripture at face value and understandably reject any attempt to avoid a straightforward interpretation. But their dogged desire to honor the righteousness of God too easily dismisses His compassion, or, at the very least, they see God as holy first and loving second.

## Looking Up

At present, much of the evangelical world has battled itself to a stalemate on the issue of divorce and, as a sad consequence, has left many suffering believers isolated and directionless. The implied message is *we know you're enduring unimaginable pain and may even be risking bodily harm, and we don't know what you should do about it. But for goodness' sake, don't seek a divorce!* Not only does this fail to offer hope or provide leadership but also creates an incubator for sin, both for the unrepentant partner and the suffering spouse. Clearly, something must be done. But what? How do we resolve the no-win scenario?

In the early 1960s, Thomas Kuhn wrote a book titled *The Structure of Scientific Revolutions*, in which he coined the term *paradigm shift*. When scientists can no longer make sense of their data using the established theories, someone stumbles upon a new perspective that sparks a scientific revolution. The facts don't change; we just change our way of looking at them.

To use a word picture, think of a path leading to a wall. In the past, we may have turned left or right to go around something blocking our progress. Turning left or right always worked in the past because the obstacles were relatively small. So we've never needed any other way of thinking. But now we've come to a wall that stretches for miles in either direction. Turning left or right will no longer solve the problem. We need a new solution. We need a new dimension to our thinking: *up*. We must climb over the wall, something we never thought to do before.

We are at an impasse. To turn left, we must either compromise righteousness or bend the Bible to sanctify our desire for mercy. To turn right, we must hold high the sanctity of marriage at the expense of compassion, forcing many thousands to choose between sin and survival. We need a new perspective—a paradigm shift. A way to view the issues in three dimensions instead of only two. We need an "up" kind of solution.

Let me propose something in the form of a question. Before you read on, pause for a few moments and think about this: *What if the legal instruments typically used to terminate a marriage could be used to redeem an unrepentant spouse and save a marriage?*

What if we could find a way to give the divorce process a redemptive purpose? What if we could engage the same biblical principles we apply to parenting and church discipline to an unrepentant spouse? What if we could, by using the spiritual and legal tools currently available, raise the stakes on marriage rather than lower our expectations? What if we could use the civil court system to give real meaning to the words *sanctity of marriage* instead of the mere lip service we offer now?

I chose the words *redemptive divorce* carefully when thinking of what to call this radically different way of thinking. The phrase is deliberately paradoxical and in some ways counterintuitive. But, as I trust you will discover, it describes the process well. In the meantime, don't let the name throw you off. This is not a book about divorce although the marriage may officially end. The wholehearted intent of this process is to save a marriage that seems to be over and in all likelihood destined for the divorce courts.

When applied correctly, this redemptive process honors the institution of marriage by taking the vows seriously. Rather than merely looking to the upright spouse to hang in there through thick and thin, it transfers responsibility for saving the marriage to the offending spouse, who in fact controls the destiny of the union. Rather than placing unrealistic expectations on the upright spouse, this tough-love approach communicates realistic expectations to the offending spouse and provides a means of genuine accountability. Redemptive divorce draws a clear line in the sand, refusing to tolerate unrepentant sin. But rather than condemn and reject the sinner, it offers hope and restoration.

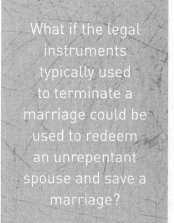

What if the legal instruments typically used to terminate a marriage could be used to redeem an unrepentant spouse and save a marriage?

The benefits for the upright spouse are many. People who are targets of verbal and emotional abuse or victims of unrepentant sin feel helpless—because they are. They helplessly watch their unions dissolve. They helplessly plead for repentance and a return to healthy, functional interaction while their spouses continue to sin without restraint. They helplessly try to restore order to homes given to chaos, and they helplessly try to shield their children from the deadly fallout of unchecked sin. But redemptive divorce places power back in the hands of the upright partner, giving him or her a means to restore genuine order to the home, real protection for the children, and the ability to plan a hopeful future.

Redemptive divorce depends entirely upon a straightforward reading of Scripture and applies tried-and-true biblical principles. To make this work, we need not twist the words of Christ or neutralize

His commands. Our shared purpose—all of us who hold high the one-flesh union God ordained from the beginning of the world and which His Son reaffirmed during His earthly ministry—is to honor His Word and to faithfully reflect His character in how we handle every aspect of life, not the least of which is the institution of marriage. Regrettably, our best intentions notwithstanding, the church has not done well in this regard. Our present paradigm makes enemies of God's compassion and His holiness instead of seeing them as they are: companions. Even worse, the current approach to failing marriages misappropriates the Lord's attributes, extending tender mercy to the oppressor while placing rigid demands for obedience on the innocent.

Far from twisting the words of Jesus or trying to find a way around His commands, this new up kind of solution to the no-win scenario clings to the righteousness of God as something to be treasured rather than circumvented. And if we are looking up as we should, the call of God to be holy as He is holy will become power in the hands of the upright spouse instead of binding him or her to the spiritual millstone of an incorrigible mate.

Redemptive divorce gives hope to the upright spouse, grace to the offending partner, and quite possibly the best opportunity for restoration of the marital union.

The temptation to take shortcuts and the opportunity for misuse are pervasive. But correctly applied, redemptive divorce gives hope to the upright spouse, grace to the offending partner, and quite possibly the best opportunity for restoration of the marital union.

## Who Needs this Book?

If you are someone like Diane, whose partner has become an enemy because of abuse or persistent, unrepentant sin, you have suffered long enough. You have endured the well-meaning exhortations of friends and family to remain faithful to your wedding day promises, you have borne the consequences of your spouse's sin, you have exhausted every means of restoration, you have loved without reservation, you have returned good for evil, and you have sacrificed your dignity and self-respect for the sake of your household. You have done well. You have done more than most would do, including the people who have not personally experienced the kind of anguish you have endured for so long. Now it's time to take your future back from the one who holds you captive to fear, shame, chaos, and hopelessness, and submit your future again to the One who rightfully owns your life.

The days ahead will not be easy. Redemptive divorce is not a quick fix. It is not a means by which you can reform or control your dysfunctional mate, nor will it heal your wounds overnight. And the faith this process requires will challenge you like nothing you have yet faced. It will, however, provide the best opportunity for your mate to surrender his or her life to God and the best way to reclaim safety and sanity for yourself and those who depend upon you. I cannot guarantee that your marriage will be saved, but if you will follow the process carefully, if you faithfully and prayerfully apply these principles, a surprising and delightful future waits for you.

If you are the friend or loved one of someone struggling to survive a dysfunctional or dangerous marriage, he or she needs you. Very likely, pain has pushed him or her beyond the ability to offer grace or even to think past the present crisis. And once your loved one has tasted the power and freedom this process offers, he or she will need you even more. Your steady support will be crucial to helping your loved one see the redemptive process through to the end.

If you are a pastor or counselor to someone stuck in a no-win marriage, redemptive divorce is a solidly biblical way to bring genuine accountability to the relationship, to offer practical help to an otherwise helpless sufferer, and to give the marriage its best chance for restoration. You will likely find the principles familiar, only applied to marriage and utilizing civil divorce proceedings in ways you may not have considered before.

The Christian family law attorney may be encouraged to take a very different role in the divorce process. Many Christian attorneys have reluctantly facilitated the divorce of Christian couples, hoping to minimize their legal and financial damage. Theirs is often a misunderstood and thankless job, and few outsiders can appreciate how helpless and conflicted they feel. One attorney in Dallas eases his emotional strain by running an adoption agency with the fees he collects from divorce cases. Others struggle to maintain a philosophical view of good and evil as they devote themselves to helping victims move on with their lives.

Redemptive divorce works best when a Christian attorney and a Christian counselor work closely together as a team. Each state has its own legal quirks, and each case is uniquely complex. The legal instruments must be honed to a razor-sharp edge to provide effective accountability to the offending partner. And if all goes well, the case will be so airtight and so compelling that the sinning spouse will see little choice but to repent and do what is right for the marriage, the children, and his or her relationship with God.

# Two

## "The Marriage Is Over!" What Does that Mean?

*A little more than two years ago, my husband left me and our two small children, Luke and Joy. He moved to a family member's house in the same town while he continues to see his mistress, who lives in a nearby state. He helps to support her, but he doesn't provide financial support for our children.*

*What should I do? The people in my church family say that I should be patient and let the Lord convict him of his sin. They have discouraged me from going to court. Should I file for child support? Should I file for divorce?*

*Please help me pray. I need the Lord's help. My husband needs to do what is right. Please pray that his mistress will realize what she's doing to our family. My children deserve a normal life instead of this.*

—KAREN

Karen's predicament is not uncommon although the details of her case are more extreme than most. She is divorced in every practical sense of the word, yet she finds herself questioning the morality of filing for divorce. Many would counsel her to accept the sad fact that her marriage is over, put the pieces of her life together, and move on. Others applaud her steadfast devotion and would counsel her against giving up the hope that her marriage might be saved. I confess that I once insisted that petitioning the court for a divorce not only precludes the hope of reconciliation but demonstrates a lack of faith in God's ability or willingness to revive a dead or dying marriage. Conversations with many counselors and family law attorneys and my examination of church history have given me a different perspective.

Those who find themselves the sole caretaker of a dead marriage almost always struggle to overcome feelings of guilt for even considering divorce. Somehow, the act of having a judge legally declare the marriage over feels disloyal, like the upright spouse is the unfaithful partner for filing divorce papers. Many cling to the hope that if they exercise enough faith or stand in belief as they pray, perhaps God will intervene. After all, He can raise the dead; certainly He can resurrect a marriage. These feelings of guilt and self-doubt are often reinforced by family, friends, and church leaders, who sincerely share this strong aversion to the divorce decree.

But why is this aversion so strong? What about the divorce decree do we find so abhorrent that we would rather allow innocent people to suffer unconscionable neglect or even unspeakable abuse? And why do we consider Karen's dead marriage still viable simply because a judge hasn't signed a decree saying that it isn't?

I see two reasons—two perspectives—that we should examine closely. First, we do not have an adequate definition of what constitutes a marriage and, therefore, divorce. Second, we have difficulty making sense of evil in a world over which God is sovereign.

## The Making of Marriage

Usually, we intuitively know whether a couple is married or not. We have an internal, unconscious set of criteria that, when satisfied, gives us the sense that a couple is genuinely united in a one-flesh union. Christians living in Western cultures, whether they realize it or not, generally see marriage resting on three pillars: *the mystical union* (marriage in the eyes of God), *the covenant* (marriage in the eyes of the community), and *legal status* (marriage in the eyes of the state). When all three pillars stand strong and true, no one questions the status of the marriage. When a couple obtains a marriage license, utters vows before a clergyman in the presence of their community, and then takes up residence together, we are satisfied on all three levels that the couple is unquestionably married. However, if any one of the three pillars becomes compromised, the legitimacy or status of the marriage comes into question, and opinions as to what makes marriage quickly diverge.

## The Mystical Union

Marriage originated with God. Long before centralized government and civil courts, long before covenant ceremonies and community celebrations, the Creator of humankind fashioned a solitary human and punctuated His creative act with the words, "It is not good." For someone reading the first two chapters of Genesis, the declaration comes like a slap in the face. God created light and called it "good" (1:4). God separated dry land from the seas and "saw that it was good" (v. 10). He covered the earth with vegetation and "saw that it was good" (v. 12). He sprinkled the heavens with stars and planets and "saw that it was good" (v. 18). He filled the sea with creatures and the air with birds and "saw that it was good" (v. 21). He fashioned a marvelous array of animals to creep, crawl, leap, and lumber and "saw that it was good" (v. 25). But of the solitary human, God said, "The man's being by himself is *not good*; I will make for him a corresponding helper" (Gen. 2:18; my translation).

After creating the man, God did something curious. He brought every order of bird and land animal to the man for naming, after which Moses states, "But for Adam, a helper corresponding to him was not found" (Gen. 2:20; my translation). We tend to think of a helper as someone subservient or secondary to another, such as an electrician's helper or perhaps a scrub nurse in an operating room. However, the Hebrew word translated *helper* in this verse is the same word used in Psalm 54:4 and throughout Hebrew poetry to describe the Lord. Far from being subservient or secondary, a helper in the Hebrew language spoke of someone indispensable. The helper Adam needed was a necessary companion without whom he could not fulfill his very reason for being. Furthermore, his helper had to be "corresponding" to or, as the literal Hebrew reads, "according to the opposite of him."[1] Humankind was incomplete without the helper, but no existing creature could suffice. So God performed an utterly unique creative miracle. Unlike each of the corresponding pairs of animals and birds He had formed from dirt (Gen. 2:19), God fashioned a woman from the man's own flesh. He breathed life into a part of the man's body and returned her to him as a mate.

Finally, the formation of Eve completed God's creation of humankind. Adam exclaimed, "Now, *at last!* She is bone of my bones, and flesh of my flesh." Moses then associates this account of human creation with the divine institution of marriage. "For this reason a man shall leave his father and his mother, and be joined to his wife; and they shall become one flesh" (Gen. 2:24). As John MacArthur explains,

"One flesh" speaks of a complete unity of parts making a whole, e.g., one cluster, many grapes (Num. 13:23) or one God in three persons (Deut. 6:4); thus this marital union was complete and whole with two people. This also implies their sexual completeness. One man and one woman constitute the pair to reproduce.[2]

In Genesis 1, Moses summarizes the creation of humanity using a common Hebrew sentence structure known as parallelism, in which subsequent lines restate the thought of the first line. The statements are understood to be synonymous.

> God created *man* in His own image,
> in the image of God He created *him*;
> *male and female* He created *them*. —v. 27 (emphasis added)

Curiously, the words *man, him, male and female,* and *them* in these verses overlap in meaning. In fact, the parallelism of this verse is so curious that Jewish tradition once held that Adam was originally hermaphroditic—that is, he had both male and female reproductive parts until separated into man and woman.[3] Of course, Moses does not use *man* to refer to Adam but to humanity. His point is this: the image of God was not fully reflected in humankind until both man and woman had been created. Like the oneness and the "threeness" of the triune God, so is the maleness and femaleness of humanity. Any thought of division is nonsensical. The joining of man and woman in marriage memorializes this completed reflection of His image, and their one-flesh sexual union is God's ordained means of reproducing humanity.

Marriage, as conceived by God, is a mystical union that transcends the laws of governments and the traditions of cultures. Jesus said, "They are no longer two, but one flesh. What therefore God has joined together, let no man separate" (Matt. 19:6). Paul used this mysterious intertwining to illustrate Christ's union with His body of believers:

> Husbands ought also to love their own wives as their own bodies. He who loves his own wife loves himself; for no one ever hated his

own flesh, but nourishes and cherishes it, just as Christ also does the church, because we are members of His body.

—Ephesians 5:28–30

While the act of sex consummates the union, it does not constitute marriage, which is why Paul cautioned believers:

Do you not know that your bodies are members of Christ? Shall I then take away the members of Christ and make them members of a prostitute? May it never be! Or do you not know that the one who joins himself to a prostitute is one body with her? For He says, "The two shall become one flesh."

—1 Corinthians 6:15–16

As commentator Thomas Constable explains: "'One flesh' is not the same as marriage. For there to be a marriage there must also be a commitment to 'leave' parents and 'cleave' to one's spouse from then on." He continues:

A newly married couple is wise to establish relative independence from both sets of parents emotionally, physically, financially, and in other ways. The couple also needs to establish commitment to one another. Cleaving resembles weaving two threads into one new piece of cloth. The word suggests the ideas of passion and permanence. In marriage a man's priorities change. Before they were primarily to his parents, but now they are primarily to his wife.[4]

While a single instance of sexual intercourse doesn't make a marriage, it can, however, sever the mystical union. After quoting God's Word from Genesis 2, Jesus said, "Whoever divorces his wife, except for [sexual] immorality, and marries another woman commits adultery" (Matt. 19:9). He undoubtedly said this to affirm the permanence of marriage against the prevailing view that the union could be dissolved on a whim; however, the sole reference to sexual immorality lets us know that in the divine mind, at least, the mystical union is severed when the marriage bed has been violated. God's righteousness does not bind a man or woman to a spouse who has been sexually unfaithful.

For some evangelicals, the mystical union is the only definition of marriage. To them, the covenant made by the couple and witnessed by the community, while essential, merely solemnizes the union. The marriage license, while equally essential, merely satisfies the state's legal requirement for documentation; it does not make the couple one. By virtue of the mystical union—marriage in the eyes of God—the two are eternally bound in a one-flesh union that cannot be broken except by sexual infidelity. Most other evangelical pastors, teachers, and counselors maintain that if the mystical union is not the exclusive definition of marriage, it is at the very least primary.

## The Covenant

Before the establishment of centralized governments, such as monarchies or republics, people looked to the patriarchs of their community for justice and order. Elder men of ancient Hebrew communities gathered at the main gate of the city or around the community well to hear disputes and debate issues in order to decide how the community would respond. One issue of primary concern to the community was the union of two people in marriage.

A young man could indicate his commitment to "leave and cleave" and enter the bond of marriage in one of three ways, according to Jewish tradition. The man could pay money to the woman's guardian, he could present a contract either to the woman's guardian or to the woman herself if she were of age, or he could have sexual intercourse with her. And as long as the pairing didn't violate any established customs or cause any potential legal complications, the union received the blessing of the community.[5]

In our day and age, we find this latter means of marriage shocking; the idea of having sexual relations before a ceremony smacks of something illegitimate. Today, when a couple begins living as husband and wife without a marriage license or a ceremony, we call it common-law marriage and tend to treat their union with polite disdain. But for most of human history and in most non-Christian cultures, both ancient and modern, cohabitation *is* marriage, and the act of sex—in any context and for any reason—consummates the couple's union (Ex. 22:16; Deut. 21:10–13; 22:28–29). While ceremony and celebration were very important community events, they merely acknowledged the union; they did not make a marriage. Nevertheless, every culture attached certain expectations to the common-law union and, even though vows were not spoken, the couple was expected to abide by the community's rules of marriage.

Of course, Hebrew culture didn't merely evolve, and its customs are anything but arbitrary. They received their standard of conduct from God. Even so, the development of ceremony and celebration in connection with marriage came a considerable time after Moses received the first five books of the Old Testament. As populations grew and societies became more complex, the need for community approval of a couple's union prior to consummation became very important. Consider, for example, the case of Boaz and Ruth.

*Ruth & Boaz* Ruth was tragically widowed during the time of the Judges, before Saul or David ruled as king and when Israel's communities looked to councils of elder men for leadership. She suddenly found herself alone and destitute, having only her widowed mother-in-law for support. Where her culture failed to offer Social Security or government assistance, the Hebrew rite of "levirate marriage" offered hope. Levirate marriage was a provision in God's Law whereby a childless widow should become the wife of her husband's nearest relative (Deut. 25:5–10). This not only protected her from poverty, but it kept the man's estate in the family.

Ruth's mother-in-law noticed that Boaz, an older man and a distant relative of Ruth's deceased husband—presumably a widower—had shown Ruth extraordinary kindness. She then told her daughter-in-law how to ask Boaz to become her "kinsman-redeemer" by way of levirate marriage.

> Now Boaz, with whose female servants you worked, is our close relative. Look, tonight he is winnowing barley at the threshing floor. So bathe yourself, rub on some perfumed oil, and get dressed up. Then go down to the threshing floor. But don't let the man know you're there until he finishes his meal. When he gets ready to go to sleep, take careful notice of the place where he lies down. Then go, uncover his legs, and lie down beside him. He will tell you what you should do.
>
> —Ruth 3:2–4 NET

Some commentators debate the significance of "uncover his legs and lie down." Some say it was merely a gesture that a man in that culture would have understood as a proposal of marriage, not unlike a man today getting down on one knee and holding out a ring. Even without a word, a woman in our culture would understand his intention. Other expositors maintain that her gesture invited Boaz to commit himself to marriage by making love to her, which would have been entirely acceptable according to Hebrew custom, even as late as AD 200.

Boaz, being an honorable gentleman, declined the invitation, knowing that his community would not have affirmed their union. The right to redeem Ruth belonged to another man, who was a closer relative of her dead husband. Boaz would have to seek the approval of the elders before taking Ruth as his wife.

The story ends happily. The other man waived his claims to Ruth and her husband's estate, which cleared the way for Boaz. But imagine the social embarrassment and legal difficulties that would have followed Boaz if he had accepted Ruth's proposal of marriage on the spot. Fortunately, this wise man of integrity understood the customs of his community. To keep his life and reputation above reproach, he sought the approval of the elders before acting. Unfortunately, very few people care as much about honor.

The primary purpose of the marriage ceremony is to formalize a covenant between the bride and groom, and between the couple and their community. The couple obtains permission to marry from the community by making a public declaration of their intent; the community gives its blessing by witnessing their contract and by celebrating their union. The covenant ceremony also places upon the community a responsibility to hold the couple to their agreement. Everyone—not just the bride and groom—holds a genuine stake in the success of the marriage. Marriage and family are essential to building and maintaining a strong society.

Many Jewish historians note that after the Jews returned to Palestine after the Exile, "the process of marriage seems to have undergone greater formalization" involving a multistaged progression from the proposal, to the contract, through a betrothal period, and culminating in the home-taking celebration. "As Jews became a dispersed minority and came into close contact with other peoples . . . , greater emphasis was placed on [marriage restrictions] as critical to preserving the covenant [between God and Abraham]."[6] Intercourse for the sake of betrothal, as it was called, presented cultural and legal difficulties that public ceremony and celebration could preclude, particularly when living among other peoples during the Exile. However, Jewish communities around the world adopted different standards. Only after the destruction of the temple in AD 70 did the Jews adopt a single custom, which they preserved in the Mishnah, the written record of rabbinic tradition.

Interestingly, the Lord never prescribed a certain ceremonial method of uniting a man and woman in matrimony. In fact, He didn't even offer a suggestion. Beyond the commitment of the man and woman to leave their respective families, cleave to each other, and consummate their commitment by becoming one flesh in sexual union, the Lord is pleased to allow us any form of ceremony and celebration as meets our needs as a culture. While He did not ordain or require a marriage ceremony, He nonetheless adds His blessing.

This is not to say that a marriage ceremony isn't extremely important. Cultures rely upon traditions because they serve a vital purpose. Having the couple commit themselves to a lifelong union in the presence of their community gives them powerful reason to remain together when they inevitably face difficulties. Given her present circumstance, Karen's question—"Should I file for divorce?"— illustrates the compelling influence of the marriage ceremony and the involvement of her community in her desire to remain faithful. Had her family, friends, and church not placed such high value on marriage, she would have probably sought a divorce the week after her husband left.

For many people, the covenant *is* marriage. The one-flesh union is a kind of contract that involves promises, terms, and conditions. David Instone-Brewer has written extensively on the subject of divorce and includes a great amount of historical, cultural, and linguistic information. However, his defense rests almost entirely on the covenantal view of marriage. He traces the vows in Christian marriage back to Ephesians 5:28–29, Jewish tradition, and Exodus 21:10 to support his view that marriage is, essentially, a covenant in the eyes of God and nothing more.

> The biblical vows have survived intact from their origins in the book of Exodus, via the Jewish marriage contracts and the letter to the Ephesians, and through to the early English marriage services, where they have remained almost unchanged for the last thousand years. The language has evolved from "love, clothe and feed" to more general terms like "love, honor and cherish," but the underlying principles have remained the same—material support and physical affection. When we marry, we make these promises to each other, and when we break them, the marriage starts to break down, because when we fail to love and honor and cherish each other, what is left?
>
> The Holy Spirit has ensured that we still make the same marriage vows that God recommended through Moses, even though the church has forgotten their origin.[7]

This view holds that marriage is a covenant between people that is ratified by God when He blesses and seals it with His Holy Spirit. Many who define marriage as a covenant believe it to be inviolable. Others like Instone-Brewer believe that a violation of the terms of the contract necessarily dissolves the covenant, both on earth and in heaven.

## Legal Status

The needs of the state are relatively simple as it relates to marriage. The courts need to know how to apply the law. Because common-law marriages complicate the state's ability to apply the law, courts rely upon two legal documents to define marriage: the marriage license and the divorce decree. These two documents declare the status of the couple's union for legal purposes. However, if the couple does not inform the government of their marital status, the court will apply its own standard, come to a conclusion, and treat them accordingly. For instance, Karen and her husband have been living apart for more than two years; therefore, the state in which they live considers them divorced. If her husband borrows money without Karen's signature, the courts will not hold her responsible for repayment because, in the eyes of the government, she is no longer his wife.

A good analogy would be birth and death certificates. A birth certificate doesn't make a baby, nor is a couple seeking permission from the state to have a child. It is merely a legal instrument that declares to the state that a new person exists. The child is very much alive and very much a person without a birth certificate; however, the courts will have a much easier time upholding justice for all concerned if they know when, where, and to whom the child was born. Similarly, a death certificate doesn't cause or sanction death; it merely documents the reality of the person's status. This legal instrument helps the state safeguard the rights of all concerned, not the least of whom is the unfortunate person who only *appears* to be dead!

Most people do not think of marriage merely in terms of its legal status. In fact, it's not uncommon for a couple to complete their wedding ceremony and return from the honeymoon only to discover that a clerical error has rendered the marriage license invalid. While the bride may be devastated by the

> As Christians, we are most concerned with how God views the couple's union.

news, a judge would likely chuckle at the irony. And let's face it; we would too.

Of the three pillars, the legal status of the marriage is the least important moral issue. As Christians, we are most concerned with how God views the couple's union. If He were to publicly announce in no uncertain terms, "Karen and her husband are no longer married in My eyes; she is free to marry another," we would care very little about how the state views their union. Nevertheless, we tend to give undue significance to the divorce decree when faced with situations like Karen's. Of all the sins committed against Karen and against the institution of marriage, we see filing for divorce as the worst sin of all. Why?

## The Problem of Evil

The presence of evil in a world over which God is still sovereign is perhaps humankind's most perplexing puzzle. The problem of evil, as it is called by philosophers, also makes divorce confusing for believers, especially as it relates to filing for a decree of divorce. Perhaps we struggle with this decision because it suggests we have given up on God.

I was three years into a four-year program, earning a masters of theology degree from Dallas Theological Seminary, when my wife suddenly left me for another man. The event came as a shock, not only emotionally but also theologically. In addition to the heartache of losing a partner for life, I found myself struggling to understand how God could allow such a thing. So I began to pray for the restoration of my marriage and had every reason to believe my prayers would be answered. Jesus promised that if we prayed in His name—that is, according to His will—the Father would grant us anything (John 16:23). Certainly, God wanted my marriage to continue, I reasoned, so I diligently prayed for reconciliation while believing I had received it (Mark 11:24). I sincerely believed that restoration was only a matter of time. Meanwhile, I pursued every practical means of putting my marriage back together, including the redemptive divorce process.

Weeks turned to months, and it became clearer with each passing day that my wife was not going to return. In fact, she demonstrated very clearly that she was committed to her present course. Eventually, the state recognized her common-law union with the other man. In other words, they were legally married, which brought the *problem of evil* very close to home. If God were sovereign, how could He permit something so contrary to His will? What of the promises about prayer Jesus offered in the upper room? Had I not prayed fervently enough or with enough faith?

God originally crafted the world, fashioned man and woman in His own image, and declared His creation good. Every physical need of the couple found ample supply in the goodness of His handiwork, their one-flesh union sated their emotional needs, and they enjoyed spiritual abundance in regular communion with God. They were "naked and were not ashamed" because they had no reason for worry or shame or doubt or sadness (Gen. 2:25). But then they chose to disobey their Creator, subjecting all of creation to the consequences of their sin. The world then became a grotesque perversion of what God had created to be good. And ever since that horrific choice in the Garden, we have been living east of Eden, banished from the goodness that God desired—and still desires—for us. Collectively and individually, we are living with the consequences of sin in a creation that does not work like God wants it to.

Even so, God has not left us alone. He made the "problem of evil" His own by becoming one of us. In the person of Jesus Christ, God

31

became a man to redeem the world, and He will eventually make it even more glorious than before. This universe will give way to "a new heaven and a new earth" (Rev. 21:1). In the meantime, God has not promised that we will remain untouched by evil or escape death. Instead, He has promised that death will not be the end and that evil will not have the final victory in the cosmic battle that rages around us. Until Jesus returns to reclaim the world from the clutches of Satan, "the whole creation groans and suffers" (Rom. 8:22), we "groan within ourselves, waiting eagerly for our adoption as sons, the redemption of our body" (Rom. 8:23), and the Holy Spirit "intercedes for us with groanings too deep for words" (Rom. 8:26).

God did not ordain marriage to end in divorce any more than He fashioned our bodies for death. Both divorce and death are an affront to His created order. Nevertheless, death is inevitable because of sin, and sometimes divorce cannot be avoided because at least one partner has chosen sin to become his or her new mate.

In time, I realized that my prayers had to change. Instead of praying for the resurrection of my dead marriage or for the revival of the future I thought should have been, I began to pray for the ability to accept the fact that my marriage had become a casualty of evil, a circumstance that God didn't like any more than I did. I began to pray for a redeemed future in whatever form God saw fit to fashion it.

## Redeeming Good After Evil

A divorce decree doesn't end a marriage any more than a death certificate ends a life; it merely declares what has already occurred. Filing for divorce does nothing more than inform the state: this marriage is over because at least one person, by virtue of his or her actions, has decided to end it. The documents also help protect the upright spouse from any more pain or abuse than already suffered as well as safeguard the interests of the children, given the circumstances.

In most cases and by most standards, the marriage is over long before anyone declares it to the state. The mystical union has been treated with contempt, and the covenant has been run through the shredder. Unfortunately, we have placed such significance on the divorce decree that, if we are not careful, we can allow it to become an instrument of denial instead of a possible means of redemption. Imagine how absurd it would be for a community to refuse a death certificate merely because no one wanted to accept that a person is dead. Meanwhile, the family of the deceased cannot move forward, feeling guilty for giving up faith in God's ability to raise the dead yet left alone to care for a corpse as though it were alive. How much better it would be if the community could surround the upright spouse and affirm him or her in the reality that the marriage is over and then commit to helping that wounded brother or sister face the future.

Fortunately, this is where the death analogy breaks down. Divorce is not death. Unlike death certificates, divorce decrees can become the means of reviving a dead marriage. Refusing to acknowledge that the marriage is over, on the other hand, will guarantee a future that no one wants.

Let's face it; usually the decree of divorce is used by angry, vindictive partners to stab at the heart of their

> A piece of paper doesn't divide what God said no man should separate. Sin does that.

wayward mate. But instead of a dagger, perhaps this legal instrument can become a scalpel. Maybe we can use the court and the process of divorce to cut out the cancer of sin and give the union a chance to recover. If so, we must recognize that marriage is indeed more than a piece of paper and that a piece of paper doesn't divide what God said no man should separate. Sin does that. And allowing habitual, unrepentant sin to continue without consequence does not honor marriage; it profanes the one-flesh union God ordained. When one partner makes a victim of the other, with or without a divorce decree, the marriage is over. Whether there is hope for the couple depends entirely upon what we choose to do next.

# Three

## The Biblical Divorce

*I have read about divorce and heard sermons about divorce, so I under-
stand what the Bible says about divorce. But I want to know, what if
you were raised in a dysfunctional home that taught you all the wrong
things about marriage, and you married when you should have remained
single? Isn't it wrong to stay in a bad marriage? Doesn't God want people
to be happy? Does He want me to waste my life on a partner who isn't
even a believer?*

*We have tried to work it out and have even been to marriage counsel-
ing. Nothing has changed, and it probably won't get better. We have both
been married before.*

*Leslie*

Citing unhappiness or boredom as grounds for divorce has been
around a long time. In fact, the right to divorce and remarry at will had
become a thorny issue around the time of Jesus as the schools of two
highly esteemed Pharisees, Hillel and Shammai, took opposing posi-
tions in the debate. While the argument focused on the interpretation
of the Old Testament—specifically Deuteronomy 24:1–4—this was
no mere squabble among theologians. The controversy had far-reach-
ing implications politically and socially.

Before Moses received the Law from God, "the fundamental principle of government was the absolute authority of the oldest male ascendant, who was the lawgiver and the judge, and whose rule over his wives, children and slaves was supreme."[1] This included the unquestioned right of the patriarch to send a wife away if he became displeased with her. Most notably, Abraham "rose early in the morning and took bread and a skin of water and gave them to Hagar, putting them on her shoulder, and gave her the boy, and sent her away" (Gen. 21:14). We know from the Scriptures that Abraham acted with the Lord's blessing; nevertheless, some rabbis took this as a precedent for the absolute right of a patriarch to marry and divorce at will.

God's Law, given at the time of Israel's entering the Promised Land, greatly curtailed the absolute power of the patriarch. Nevertheless, the patriarch's power over the family and his influence in the community remained the backbone of Hebrew society through the rise and fall of governments and foreign invaders. By the time of Jesus, this centuries-old mainstay of Jewish culture appeared to be in peril. Monogamy had replaced polygamy, the traditional measure of a patriarch's status. Autonomy had given way to the strict laws of the Roman emperor Augustus, which legally recognized patriarchal power but regulated marriage and family like no other government had. And more than anything, it was this intrusion of Roman law into Hebrew custom that divided the Sadducees from the Pharisees, and the school of Hillel from that of Shammai.

Much like today, some Jews interpreted the words of the Old Testament rigidly, others loosely, and some with a certain amount of—shall we say?—creative license! Sadducees took an inflexible approach to Scripture and remained theologically conservative, recognizing only the first five books of the Old Testament and nothing more. They held a lower view of the rest of the Old Testament—the books of history, wisdom, and prophecy—and utterly rejected the traditions of the Pharisees. By accepting only the Pentateuch, the Sadducees could ignore the prohibitions of the prophets and the warnings of history that Israel should avoid partnership with pagan nations. This rigidity freed them to cooperate with Rome and enjoy the financial and political rewards of collaboration.

The Pharisees, on the other hand, interpreted the Scriptures loosely and amplified God's instruction with a host of traditions. They became theologically innovative in order to sanctify their strict separation from Rome—and from anything else that wasn't Jewish. Preserving the patriarch's autonomy and safeguarding his power against Gentile intrusion ranked high among their concerns. However, Hillel took his innovations in a direction that would have pleased the Sadducees, especially in regard to marriage.

When a man takes a wife and marries her, and it happens that she finds no favor in his eyes because he has found some indecency in her, and he writes her a certificate of divorce and puts it in her hand and sends her out from his house, and she leaves his house and goes and becomes another man's wife, and if the latter husband turns against her and writes her a certificate of divorce and puts it in her hand and sends her out of his house, or if the latter husband dies who took her to be his wife, then her former husband who sent her away is not allowed to take her again to be his wife, since she has been defiled; for that is an abomination before the Lord, and you shall not bring sin on the land which the LORD your God gives you as an inheritance. —Deuteronomy 24:1–4

The Hebrew phrase translated "some indecency" is literally "a matter of nakedness," which had long been a Jewish idiom for "a shameful matter." The vivid picture of nudity reflects the naked shame of Adam and Eve after their sin against God (Gen. 3:7, 10–11). While Shammai interpreted this phrase to mean nothing other than sexual sin, especially adultery, Hillel noticed something peculiar about the inclusion of the term *a matter of*, which also meant *a cause for*.

Hillel asked, why did Moses use the phrase "cause of sexual immorality" when he could simply have said "sexual immorality?" Hillel reasoned that the seemingly superfluous word *cause* must refer to another, different ground for divorce, and since the other ground is simply called a "cause," he concluded that it meant any cause.

Hillel therefore thought that two types of divorce were taught in Deuteronomy 24:1: one for "sexual immorality" (adultery) and one they named "Any Cause."[2]

## Jesus on Divorce

Both Shammai and Hillel understood Deuteronomy 24:1–4 as God's sanctioning divorce; however, they disputed what gave a man—and not a woman—the right to send his spouse away. When the extremely popular rabbi from Galilee arrived in Jerusalem and began teaching multitudes of Jews, the Sadducees and the two schools of Pharisees naturally wondered which viewpoint Jesus would embrace (Matt. 16:1; 22:15, 34–35; Luke 11:53–54). They especially wanted to know where He stood on the issue of divorce: "Some Pharisees came to Jesus, testing Him and asking, 'Is it lawful for a man to divorce his wife for any reason at all?'" (Matt. 19:3) The last phrase is literally, "according to any cause?" In other words, *Do You agree with Hillel's 'any cause' interpretation of Deuteronomy 24:1, or do You side with Shammai's?*

The Pharisees had earlier tried to trap Jesus in a controversy over

Caesar's tax: "Tell us then, what do You think? Is it lawful to give a poll-tax to Caesar, or not?" (Matt. 22:17). An answer in the affirmative put Jesus on the side of the Sadducees, who sought wealth and power through collaboration with Rome. A negative reply aligned Him with the Pharisees, who exploited the people for political and financial gain.

Jesus, in His own ingenious way, refused to be manipulated by anyone's agenda and turned the situation into an opportunity to advance His own. Whenever tested in this manner, He answered the question from an oblique angle, which typically exposed the flawed perspective of His challengers. The religious leaders saw the poll tax dilemma as an issue of loyalty, either to Rome or Israel. Jesus, however, exposed their limited, worldly perspective. God does not ask us to choose between Rome and Israel but between wealth and righteousness. "Render to Caesar the things that are Caesar's; and to God the things that are God's" (Matt. 22:21).

Similarly, when Jesus answered the question concerning the moral grounds for divorce, He sided with neither Shammai nor the Hillel, choosing instead to expose their flawed perspective. His teaching included three distinct points, which I will present in reverse order.

## Motivation for Marriage

One's motivation should be to remain in marriage rather than looking for a way to escape.

> The disciples said to Him, "If the relationship of the man with his wife is [not to be broken except in cases of sexual immorality], it is better not to marry." But He said to them, "Not all men can accept this statement, but only those to whom it has been given. For there are eunuchs who were born that way from their mother's womb;

and there are eunuchs who were made eunuchs by men; and there are also eunuchs who made themselves eunuchs for the sake of the kingdom of heaven. He who is able to accept this, let him accept it."
—Matthew 19:10–12

By the time of Jesus, divorce for any cause had become widely accepted. Though most religious leaders thought very little of the man who exercised this patriarchal right,[3] the any-cause divorce was increasingly common among Jews. To illustrate the concept of commitment, Jesus drew upon a familiar sight in those days: the eunuch. The defining characteristic of a eunuch is castration, after which a man can neither procreate nor, in that culture, marry. Some were born in this condition, some were surgically altered, still others chose the eunuch's way of life, either literally or figuratively.[4] In this way, Jesus took the choice for singleness, better not to marry, to the extreme.

His word picture illustrates the fact that one does not experiment with becoming a eunuch. In the literal sense of the word, the choice to become a eunuch is permanent. In the figurative, one chooses a permanent way of life for the sake of focused dedication to ministry. Everyone understands the lifelong implications of becoming a eunuch, especially if it involves castration. Similarly, the lifelong implications of marriage should be no surprise to anyone. The Creator communicated the parameters from the very beginning of human existence and has given men and women the freedom to choose. Therefore, one should not enter marriage with one foot out the door.

## Restrictions on Remarriage

Deuteronomy 24:1–4 was not given for the purpose of sanctioning divorce but to keep the practice of divorce and remarriage from becoming legalized wife-swapping.

[The Pharisees] said to Him, "Why then did Moses command to give her a certificate of divorce and send her away?" He said to them, "Because of your hardness of heart Moses permitted you to divorce your wives; but from the beginning it has not been this way. And I say to you, whoever divorces his wife, except for immorality, and marries another woman commits adultery." —Matthew 19:7–9

If Hillel's interpretation demonstrates anything, it's the desire to sin with God's blessing. And the practice is as old as the Old Testament. The rabbis found in Deuteronomy 24:1–4 divine permission to divorce, which missed the point of the passage entirely. The instruction doesn't comment on the morality of divorce at all; it prohibited remarriage of former partners in a culture where divorces were presumed to be taking place already. The instruction prevented men from divorcing their wives temporarily for the purpose of sleeping with other men's wives.

We cannot make too much of the fact that God didn't prohibit divorce outright when establishing the nation of Israel. Without approving other practices we find unsavory today, such as polygamy, concubinage, and slavery, the Lord didn't terminate them either. In fact, other Old Testament laws assumed these to be common practice and merely kept them in check (Ex. 21:1–11). Why He didn't choose to terminate behavior we now understand to be sinful is beside the point. For reasons only the Lord can know, He chose to reveal truth progressively over time. And we cannot assume He approves of something simply because He has chosen to remain silent about it. Jesus corrected the Pharisees' use of the word *command* with an important clarification. God didn't *command* anyone to divorce; He merely permitted the practice, much like He permitted polygamy, concubinage, and slavery, practices that He looked upon with even less favor.

## Marriage Is a Mystical Union

Marriage in the eyes of God is more than a mere covenant between people; it is a mystical union.

> Some Pharisees came to Jesus, testing Him and asking, "Is it lawful for a man to divorce his wife for any reason at all?" And He answered and said, "Have you not read that He who created them from the beginning made them male and female, and said, 'For this reason a man shall leave his father and mother and be joined to his wife, and the two shall become one flesh'? So they are no longer two, but one flesh. What therefore God has joined together, let no man separate."
> —Matthew 19:3–6

Before answering the Pharisees' question, Jesus pointed to God's creative act and divine decree to establish a principle that predated the laws given to Israel in Canaan. The rabbis had lost sight of God's design for marriage. They had downgraded matrimony to mere covenant and reduced women to mere chattel. Take note of what—or more appropriately, *who*—binds a couple together in the eyes of Jesus: not a covenant, not a ceremony, but God. Whereas people may have arranged the pairing, contracted the betrothal, performed the ceremony, celebrated the nuptials, and even consummated the union, "God has joined together" a man and wife. The Creator intended for one man and one woman to be joined for life in an unbreakable, mystical union.

## Raising the Stakes on Marriage

Earlier in His ministry, Jesus commented on the teaching of the rabbis concerning the Law and then offered His clarification as the divine

Author. "Do not think that I came to abolish the Law or the Prophets; I did not come to abolish but to fulfill" (Matt. 5:17). He then took the opportunity to breathe new life into some Old Testament laws and to correct the teaching of the Pharisees. Note how He continues in Matthew chapter 5 as He presented His lessons:

- "You have heard . . ." (v. 21), "But I say to you . . ." (v. 22), followed by teaching on murder and resentment.
- "You have heard . . ." (v. 27), "but I say to you . . ." (v. 28), followed by teaching on adultery and lust.
- "It was said . . ." (v. 31), "but I say to you . . ." (v. 32), followed by teaching on divorce and fidelity.
- "You have heard . . ." (v. 33), "But I say to you . . ." (v. 34), followed by teaching on vows and integrity.
- "You have heard . . ." (v. 38), "But I say to you . . ." (v. 39), followed by teaching on justice and kindness.
- "You have heard . . ." (v. 43), "But I say to you . . ." (v. 44), followed by teaching on fair play and grace.

In each case, Jesus extended the application of the Law given through Moses to include what the rabbis had omitted. Furthermore, He amplified the divine revelation in the Old Testament to reveal the full measure of God's standards. Not only must we refrain from murder, but we must also avoid hatred. Not only is adultery an abomination, so is lust.

His third point clarified God's view on marriage and divorce:

It was said, "Whoever sends his wife away, let him give her a certificate of divorce"; but I say to you that everyone who divorces his wife, except for the reason of unchastity, makes her commit adultery; and whoever marries a divorced woman commits adultery. —Matthew 5:31–32

While Old Testament law merely placed restrictions on divorce without prohibiting the practice, Jesus raised the standard to match God's original ideal. This is not to suggest that the Lord changed His stance, any more than suggesting that He was in favor of lust when prohibiting adultery or of hatred when outlawing murder. While the laws of the Old Testament reflect God's righteous character, they were primarily intended to regulate the public affairs of a nation, much like the laws of our own government. But we generally understand that a person must be more than merely law-abiding to be considered moral. Obedience to the law is a *minimum* standard. The rabbis in Jesus' day not only reduced righteousness to mere obedience to the Law, but they also played clever word games with Scripture to lower the standard even further!

Jesus was not content to leave the standard of righteousness where the rabbis had placed it. Instead of quibbling over jots and tittles in the Law, He commanded us to gaze into the character of the Father. Rather than settle for the minimum acceptable allowance, He challenged us to seek His kingdom and His righteousness, promising that if we do, all of our needs and all of our problems will be resolved in time. On the other hand, we can never sate our appetites or resolve our difficulties by ignoring His kingdom or rejecting His righteousness.

Marriage indeed is a contract between people, but that's not all. It is more. It is a union sealed and celebrated by God. The man and woman are joined by His sovereign decree, not by the authority of a clergyman or a church or public official. These earthly authorities merely attest to what God has done. When a man and woman commit to "leave," "cleave," and then consummate their union in the intimate, one-flesh act of sexual intercourse, they are joined in the eyes of God. And the words of Jesus weigh heavy with menacing gravity: "But I say to you that everyone who divorces his wife, except for the reason of [sexual immorality], makes her commit adultery; and whoever marries a divorced woman commits adultery" (Matt. 5:32).

Because Jesus used hyperbole in Matthew 5:29–30, having put lust on par with adultery, we can be reasonably certain 5:32 is another instance of dramatic overstatement for effect. He did not intend for His affirmation of marriage to stigmatize the innocent spouse in an unwanted divorce, but to demonstrate that a certificate of divorce on earth doesn't change God's view of the marriage. It is *God's* view of marriage that counts, not the blessing of community or the opinion of the courts. And here, Jesus taught that sexual immorality (*porneia*) severs the mystical union in the eyes of God.

The Greek word *porneia* is an umbrella term for a broad range of sexual sin, not just adultery. If He had wanted to limit this to adultery, He could have chosen the very common, more specific term *moicheia*. But He elected to use a term that originally stemmed from the idea of prostitution and eventually encompassed a range of illicit sexual activities, including adultery, homosexuality, incest, bestiality, and child molestation.[5]

Jesus' point is clear. While marriage is a mystical union—more than a mere covenant between people—it can be broken by profaning the intimacy that consummated it.

## Paul on Divorce

The troubled church in Corinth lay in the shadow of the temple of Aphrodite, which loomed nineteen hundred feet overhead at the summit of the Acro-corinth and where thousands of female prostitutes enticed worshipers from the farthest reaches of the Roman Empire. So infamous was this city's reputation that Aristophanes coined the word *corinthianize* to mean "to practice immorality."[6] Perhaps no city on earth presented a greater challenge to Christian marriage than the harbor town of Corinth. In response to several questions concerning marriage in the presence of so much temptation and sin, Paul declared,

> But to the married I give instructions, not I, but the Lord, that the wife should not leave her husband (but if she does leave, she must remain unmarried, or else be reconciled to her husband), and that the husband should not divorce his wife. —1 Corinthians 7:10–11

The members of the church in Corinth wanted to know if married Christians should remain married or pursue a life of single celibacy, like Paul. To this specific application, Paul applied the timeless instruction of Jesus that marriage is a lifetime commitment. On the other hand, he does appear to allow for long-term separation, presumably for reasons other than sexual immorality. Unfortunately, he did not elaborate. Paul merely stated that the woman must remain single in this circumstance. While we must avoid too much speculation, one must wonder why he would speak of the woman this way and not the man. Perhaps to allow for separation in abusive situations?

Having reviewed the teaching of Christ on marriage, Paul went on to address a specific issue that the Lord did not. The Pharisees' question concerned the morality of someone choosing divorce, not the innocent partner of someone choosing to leave. The apostle stated flatly, "The brother or the sister is not under bondage in such cases" (1 Cor. 7:15). After all, what is the abandoned partner to do? He or she cannot be held responsible for the sin of another. Furthermore, "not under bondage" here is parallel to Paul's thought in 1 Corinthians 7:39–40, which means the abandoned partner is "free to be married to whom she (or he) wishes." Paul presumes the unfaithful partner is not a believer, but the instruction is applicable to any abandoned spouse.

## Good, Old-Fashioned Divorce

So where does that leave us? A straightforward reading of Scripture—one that rejects arguments from silence and refuses to harmonize the teaching of Christ with our desires—indicates that God releases a person from the bond of marriage only under very limited circumstances: sexual immorality and abandonment. However, does that leave the partner of a wayward man or woman without recourse? Must an emotionally and verbally trampled woman remain locked up with her abuser? Must the husband of a substance-abusing woman allow her self-destruction to pull the whole family into the grave after her? Must a believer merely hope for the best as a spouse's habitual, unrepentant sin continues to desecrate the marriage and potentially scar the children for life? Unfortunately, our present way of thinking would offer a reluctant and apologetic yes. However, God shouts, "No! Absolutely not!" He gave us the bond of marriage as a blessing, not a curse. The permanence of marriage was never intended to insulate the unrepentant sinner from the consequences of his or her sin. On the contrary, the loss of one's family can become a powerful motivation to turn from sin and do what is right. A specific example from the corporate world is compelling.

Many counselors and recovering substance abusers will agree that, presently, the fear of losing one's family does little to motivate a spiraling addict to get help. The potential loss of a job, however, remains a powerful incentive to enter rehabilitation. Consequently, most top corporations have adopted a strict drug abuse and alcoholism policy along with an equally strong employee assistance program (EAP). These company-sponsored programs offer counseling and rehabilitation in exchange for probation. After just one infraction of the company's substance abuse policy, the employee is given a choice between firing and the EAP. And failure to complete the program or falling into a relapse automatically leads to termination.

On the surface, it would appear that addicts are more motivated to save their careers than their families, but there remains another possibility. Corporations make their expectations clearly understood and consistently back them with predictable action. Addicts listen to their employers not because they value career more than family but because they hope to avoid suffering genuine consequences and fear what their companies will do. The upright spouse doesn't have that power when his or her church encourages passivity in response to unrepentant sin. Ironically, in their genuine desire to encourage godliness on the part of the upright spouse, Christian leaders counsel very ungodlike actions in response to a wayward partner's marriage-destroying choices.

The early church fathers didn't make this mistake. But then, they didn't see divorce quite like we do today. They understood that a marriage is killed by unrepentant sin, not by a piece of paper. They also recognized the redemptive power of a divorce decree, one that can potentially pull a dead marriage from the ash heap and give it new life.

> The permanence of marriage was never intended to insulate the unrepentant sinner from the consequences of his or her sin.

If anyone could be called hardnosed on the issue of divorce, it would be the Ante-Nicene Fathers, men who taught and wrote after the death of the last apostle and before Constantine legalized Christianity in AD 313. They so believed in the permanence of the mystical union that they would not allow remarriage under any circumstance.[7] However, they recognized the necessity of divorce in response to unrepentant sin. Some even insisted that divorce was the duty of the upright spouse as the best means of turning his or her mate from behavior that destroys a marriage.

*The Shepherd of Hermas* became one of the most popular Christian documents in the early church. Written around AD 160, it influenced believers much like John Bunyan's *Pilgrim's Progress* does today, and it quickly became something of a manual for church administration and discipline.[8] In this imaginative dialogue with a messenger from heaven, the Pastor of Hermas asks several questions.

I said to him, "Sir, permit me to ask you a few questions." "Say on," said he. And I said to him, "Sir, if any one has a wife who trusts in the Lord, and if he detect her in adultery, does the man sin if he continue to live with her?" And he said to me, "As long as he remains ignorant of her sin, the husband commits no transgression in living with her. But if the husband know that his wife has gone astray, and if the woman does not repent, but persists in her fornication, and yet the husband continues to live with her, he also is guilty of her crime, and a sharer in her adultery." And I said to him, "What then, sir, is the husband to do, if his wife continue in her vicious practices?" And he said, "The husband should put her away, and remain by himself. But if he put his wife away and marry another, he also commits adultery." And I said to him, "What if the woman put away should repent, and wish to return to her husband: shall she not be taken back by her husband?" And he said to me, "Assuredly.

If the husband does not take her back, he sins, and brings a great sin upon himself; for he ought to take back the sinner who has repented. But not frequently. For there is but one repentance to the servants of God. In case, therefore, that the divorced wife may repent, the husband ought not to marry another, when his wife has been put away. In this matter man and woman are to be treated exactly in the same way. Moreover, adultery is committed not only by those who pollute their flesh, but by those who imitate the heathen in their actions. Wherefore if any one persists in such deeds, and repents not, withdraw from him, and cease to live with him; otherwise, you are a sharer in his sin. Therefore has the injunction been laid on you, that you should remain by yourselves, both man and woman, for in such persons repentance can take place.[9]

Justin Martyr, writing around the same time, affirmed the choice of a Christian woman to divorce her "intemperate husband."

For she, considering it wicked to live any longer as a wife with a husband who sought in every way means of indulging in pleasure contrary to the law of nature, and in violation of what is right, wished to be divorced from him. And when she was overpersuaded by her friends, who advised her still to continue with him, in the idea that some time or other her husband might give hope of amendment, she did violence to her own feeling and remained with him. But when her husband had gone into Alexandria, and was reported to be conducting himself worse than ever, she—that she might not, by continuing in matrimonial connection with him, and by sharing his table and his bed, become a partaker also in his wickednesses and impieties—gave him what you call a bill of divorce, and was separated from him.[10]

Tertullian, a contemporary of Justin Martyr and the writer of *Hermas*, exhorted upright spouses to pursue divorce in response to "adulteries," which he defined as any sin that made a Christian turn away from Christ.

> Well, then, what is a husband to do in your sect, if his wife commit adultery? Shall he keep her? But your own apostle, you know, does not permit "the members of Christ to be joined to a harlot." Divorce, therefore, when justly deserved, has even in Christ a defender.[11]

He then urged upright partners to devote themselves to praying on behalf of their wayward spouses.

We do not have an unsympathetic God. He knows the heartache of trying to love a spouse who is in love with sin. He has experienced this betrayal because He, too, knows the pain of divorce. His wife, of course, was the nation of Israel, much the same as the church is the bride of Christ. He loved His chosen nation but could no longer be the doting husband He desired to be. Israel's preference for sin over the marriage made that impossible. And like most wayward spouses, she wanted both her sin and the marriage. However, the Lord could not permit His spouse to treat Him so disrespectfully or allow continued sin to pollute their marriage.

> Then the LORD said to [Jeremiah] in the days of Josiah the king, "Have you seen what faithless Israel did? She went up on every high hill and under every green tree, and she was a harlot there. I thought, 'After she has done all these things she will return to Me'; but she did not return, and her treacherous sister Judah saw it. And I saw that for all the adulteries of faithless Israel, I had sent her away and given

her a writ of divorce, yet her treacherous sister Judah did not fear; but she went and was a harlot also. Because of the lightness of her harlotry, she polluted the land and committed adultery with stones and trees. Yet in spite of all this her treacherous sister Judah did not return to Me with all her heart, but rather in deception," declares the LORD. —Jeremiah 3:6–10)

Clearly, God's motivation for divorcing the northern kingdom of Israel was twofold. First, He hoped that turning them over to their sin would cause them to value their marriage and eventually return to Him. Second, He hoped Israel's painful divorce would serve as a warning to the southern kingdom of Judah.

The Lord used the genuine threat of divorce as a tool for redemption. Yet somehow, centuries later, we have come to mistake passivity for mercy and have adopted the notion that a divorce decree is necessarily destructive to the mystical union. On the contrary, a divorce decree, if used wisely, can be the only remaining hope of reviving a dead marriage.

# Four

## When Love Has
## to Get Tough

*My wife, Joanne, left our family and had an affair in which she lived with the other man for nearly a year. During that time, I tried everything to get her to leave him and commit to working on our marriage, but she stubbornly refused. I finally gave up and contacted a lawyer. Since then, she has been saved (for which I am genuinely happy) and wants to work on our marriage. I have been told this several times, only to find the other man still in the picture. I don't know that I can trust her. I don't know that she won't keep playing this game.*

*I want to file for divorce, but I am so confused. I'm afraid no matter what I do, I won't make a right decision, so I haven't made any at all. All I know is that I can't trust her, and I don't want to be in a marriage where I have to wonder about her faithfulness all the time.*

*Nick*

Nick's ordeal has given him every reason to be cautious and confused. On the surface, it appears his prayers have been answered and his marriage is on track to reconciliation, yet his instincts have sounded the alarm and his common sense tells him to listen. He should not ignore his disquiet. Nick's response to Joanne's yearlong love affair with sin not only prolonged her estrangement, but it made reconciliation more difficult for both of them.

After his wife left to live with another man, Nick's church encouraged him to remain steadfast and pray that she would come to her senses. The underlying presumption was that his rock-solid faithfulness would eventually melt her heart, and Joanne would come running back into his arms. And for more than a year, Nick prayed and waited. While a passive response to unrepentant sin may appear to be godly, it is in fact anything but godlike. The Lord is certainly gracious and merciful, but He never remains passive when His people reject Him in favor of sin. Several principles explain why passivity is the *least* loving response we can adopt and the *least effective* means of restoring a relationship broken by sin.

## Why Love Must Be Active

An old folk legend claims that a frog dropped into a kettle of boiling water will immediately recognize the danger to his life and waste no time leaping out. However, a frog placed in a kettle at room temperature will happily continue to bask as the water is slowly heated, even to the point of boiling. The legend has become a standard illustration for the mortal danger of gradual change.

### Passivity Camouflages a Trap

Passivity allows the sinner to gradually and comfortably enter Satan's snare.

Sin is a trap that hypnotizes its victim into thinking that all is well. Convinced that one sin caused no harm, the wayward spouse rationalizes his or her decision. Meanwhile, Satan works overtime to insulate his prey from reality and to provide an opportunity to take sin a step further. Gradually, bad behavior seems less and less bad until the wayward spouse is capable of astounding evil with little or no feelings of remorse. It's not uncommon for the deluded spouse to become convinced that his or her partner is ultimately responsible for the sin and, in many cases, that the destructive behavior is actually good for the family!

Whereas truth frustrates this gradual twisting of the mind, passivity allows Satan greater opportunity to isolate and deceive his prey. The wayward spouse needs, more than anything, a shocking dose of reality. The most loving response is to turn up the heat so that he or she will sense the danger and leap out.

## Passivity Reinforces Sinful Behavior

Passivity reinforces the false promise of sin that we can do whatever we want without suffering negative consequences.

As Eve gazed at the forbidden fruit hanging within easy reach, she saw that it was "good for food, and that it was a delight to the eyes" (Gen. 3:6). A serpent saw her longing gaze and moved a little closer. "You surely will not die!" (v. 4). His words contradicted her Creator's stern warning; nevertheless, she and her husband swallowed Satan's poisonous lie. And from that moment on, nothing would ever be the same. Within hours, the couple stood trembling as God explained how they would experience the consequences of disobedience. "Death" would not come immediately. Worse, death would painfully distort all of creation; death would come with sudden, unexpected certainty; and death would carry the soul to yet another kind of death, an eternal death too horrific to describe.

Imagine if, instead, God had remained passive and silent. At lunchtime the following day, Adam and Eve return to the forbidden tree to find the serpent lounging in its branches, wearing a contented smile. "See? What did I tell you? There you stand, quite alive! Take off that silly fig leaf underwear and have another delicious meal—on me."

Fortunately, the Lord didn't remain passive. Moved by love, He confronted Adam and Eve, opened their eyes to the consequences of their disobedience, and then cast them out of the Garden to limit their sin (Gen. 3:22–24). His righteous anger reaffirmed His earlier warning that eternal life and disobedience cannot coexist. Sin leads to death. It's a fundamental law of the universe that's as predictable and as certain as gravity.

Remaining passive while someone balances precariously on the edge of a skyscraper is not love. A wayward spouse needs intervention, not the casual affirmation of a passive response to sin.

## Passivity Allows Sin to Harm Others

Passivity allows the destructive consequences of sin to devastate the innocent.

Sin is a fire that destroys everything it touches. Substance abuse, rage, violence, sexual immorality, abandonment, neglect—any sin that burns out of control affects everyone, especially children. And a passive response to unrepentant sin is like standing idle while an arsonist sets fire to the people we love.

## Passivity Undermines Respect

Passivity undermines a crucial element of any healthy relationship: respect.

In his book *Love Must Be Tough*, Dr. James Dobson warns that nothing destroys a romantic relationship quicker than passivity and appeasement. On the other hand, Dobson assures us:

Successful marriages usually rest on a foundation of *accountability* between husbands and wives. They reinforce responsible behavior in one another by a divinely inspired system of checks and balances. In its absence, one party may gravitate toward abuse, insult, accusation, and ridicule of the other, while his or her victim placidly wipes away the tears and mutters with a smile, "Thanks, I needed that!"[1]

## Love that Is Tough

Unlike passivity, a proactive response to unrepentant sin reflects the character of God. He is relentlessly loving yet utterly uncompromising when it comes to behavior that undermines our relationship. Similarly, our loving response to sin must come from a place of strength, which begins with a clear understanding of who we are and what behavior we find acceptable.

Drs. Henry Cloud and John Townsend popularized the concept of boundaries to describe how we can establish and maintain healthy relationships. At first blush, the term sounds adversarial, but it is not. Boundaries are not barriers; they are merely lines that define areas of responsibility.

Boundaries define us. They define *what is me* and *what is not me*. A boundary shows me where I end and someone else begins, leading me to a sense of ownership.

The concept of boundaries comes from the very nature of God. God defines himself as a distinct, separate being, and he is responsible for himself. He defines and takes responsibility for his personality by telling us what he thinks, feels, plans, allows, will not allow, likes, and dislikes.[2]

In the world of relationships, boundaries are not optional. Where there are no boundaries, there is no relationship. Perhaps an illustration will help.

When you purchase a parcel of land, a survey defines where your property ends and where someone else's begins. And the deed gives you exclusive right to determine what happens on your property. Imagine, then, a neighbor knocked down your fence and began laying a foundation for an addition to his house in your backyard.

"What are you doing?" you ask.

Your neighbor barely looks up from his blueprints to answer, "I don't have enough room for my auto collection, so I'm building a bigger garage."

"But this is *my* backyard!" you protest.

"I know," he replies. "And it's perfect for my needs. Now, go away and leave me alone; I have work to do."

Clearly, the neighbor has little or no respect for your property line because he has no respect for you as a person. Spiritual boundaries are less visible, yet no less real. Boundaries are interpersonal property lines that communicate to others who we are and how they can best relate to us. Boundaries define what we like and dislike, what behavior draws us closer or pushes us away, and how much effort or time we are willing to invest in others. Boundaries also define the limits to which we are willing to accept hurtful conduct.

Passivity in response to the neighbor's callous disregard for you as a person teaches him that respect is not necessary. In fact, it gives him permission to ignore you completely as he takes or does anything he wants. In other words, his failure to acknowledge and respect your boundary proves that a relationship doesn't even exist. You are a nonperson to him.

A proactive response, on the other hand, establishes a relationship. When he experiences negative consequences for crossing the property line, he quickly learns that he must negotiate for what he wants. That requires communication, cooperation, a desire for mutual satisfaction, a willingness to give and receive honor—a relationship! A passive response, on the other hand, denies him the opportunity to fulfill our most fundamental reason for being: healthy interaction with one another and with God.

Unrepentant sin must be confronted aggressively. The wayward spouse has chosen to sacrifice his or her marriage for the sake of a love affair with sin, such as drug or alcohol addiction, adultery, compulsive gambling, verbal abuse, or any other activity that makes a victim of the other partner. This willful violation of boundaries says, in effect, *You don't matter, and our relationship is less important than what I want.* Passivity responds, *I agree with you!* Tough love, on the other hand, reestablishes the boundaries that unrepentant sin has violated or erased.

## God's Redemptive Divorce

When God called Abram to leave kith and kin for "the land which I will show you" (Gen. 12:1) and to cleave to Him exclusively, He established a covenant with a future nation. God and the Hebrew people became husband and wife. Ever the faithful husband, He nurtured her, led her, protected her, and demanded nothing in return except exclusive devotion to Him. Israel, however, did not remain faithful. She worshiped other deities and received favors from those who hated God. And when she did worship Him, it was a halfhearted, hypocritical affection that left Him cold (Amos 5:21–24). She despised what He values and pursued what He detests.

The Lord tried everything. He sent counselors, but she rejected them. (Actually, she killed them!) He allowed the consequences of her sin to affect her. He pleaded, warned, withdrew affection, and even allowed her other lovers to beat her. Yet nothing would turn Israel from the self-destructive path she had chosen. His wife remained incorrigibly sinful. Eventually, she left Him no other choice than to put her away—to divorce her. Perhaps this drastic message of tough love would get through.

To illustrate His love relationship with Israel, God chose Hosea, a prophet whose name means "salvation," and instructed him to choose a wife who would eventually pursue adulterous affairs. "So he went and took Gomer the daughter of Diblaim" (Hos. 1:3).

In the beginning, it would seem the couple enjoyed a normal marriage. Gomer conceived and bore a son who was undoubtedly Hosea's, as the phrase "bore him a son" makes clear (v. 3). But the Hebrew is ambiguous concerning the other two children, which leaves us to wonder. Eventually, Gomer's sin became very evident. She openly pursued illicit relationships and benefited financially from her paramours. Hosea then drew upon his own anguish to deliver the Lord's message to the upright citizens of Israel. His oracle provides a model of tough love, which requires no fewer than five specific actions.

## Name the Sin

First, tough love names the sin and holds the wayward partner solely responsible for his or her choices. Unfortunately, appearing to be judgmental has become the unforgivable sin of our time. To call attention to someone else's destructive behavior is often considered arrogant, hypocritical, or at the very least, rude. After all, Jesus did say, "Do not judge, and you will not be judged; and do not condemn, and you will not be condemned" (Luke 6:37) and "Why do you look at the speck that is in your brother's eye, but do not notice the log that is in your own eye?" (Matt. 7:3).

Yet Jesus also instructed His followers:

> If your brother sins, go and show him his fault in private; if he listens to you, you have won your brother. But if he does not listen to you, take one or two more with you, so that by the mouth of two or three witnesses every fact may be confirmed. If he refuses to listen to them, tell it to the church; and if he refuses to listen even to the church, let him be to you as a Gentile and a tax collector. —Matthew 18:15–17

In this context, the term *Gentiles* referred to those who did not worship God, and *tax collectors* were Jews who had abandoned their faith for the sake of wealth. Jesus didn't teach His followers to treat Gentiles and tax collectors cruelly. After all, He came to redeem sinners. Far from cruel or hypocritically judgmental, calling someone's destructive behavior *sin* is the first step toward reconciliation.

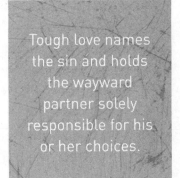

Tough love names the sin and holds the wayward partner solely responsible for his or her choices.

God's plan to redeem His wife, Israel, began when he determined to "strip her naked" and "expose her" (Hos. 2:3). The phrases are poetic, not literal.[3] To expose someone's nakedness is to prove him or her guilty of sin. The Lord brought specific charges against Israel using terms and phrases commonly associated with a Hebrew writ of divorce, and His legal complaint named each persistent, repetitive sin. His indictment also explained how her sin destroyed the marriage covenant (Hos. 2:2, 5–8; 4:1–3).

Unlike people, God is completely sinless. The mere suggestion that His behavior caused Israel to sin is laughable. Earthly husbands and wives, however, frequently attempt to shift responsibility for their sinful behavior onto their partners. Batterers claim to be provoked. Controllers contend that doubt or suspicion make their domination necessary. Substance abusers blame others for their dependency. Adulterers point to the neglect of their spouses as the reason for cheating. This blame-shifting escape goes all the way back to the Garden, where Adam pointed the finger at his wife and she, in turn, charged the serpent. The Lord anticipated this response from Israel and took a strong stand on the issue: "Yet let no one find fault, and let none offer reproof; for your people are like those who contend with the priest" (Hos. 4:4).

No mere mortal can ever claim to be completely above reproach; however, no sin—regardless of how serious or how chronic—justifies the sin of another person. No one is compelled to pursue evil. The responsibility for wrongdoing belongs exclusively to the person choosing destructive behavior. While the upright spouse must be willing to address his or her own contribution to the breakdown of the marriage, it must never be a condition of the other person's doing what is right, and it must never be a precondition to restoring a broken relationship. There will be time enough for addressing past wrongs after *both* partners are committed to the union and the marriage is back on track with the help of a competent counselor.

## Clarify the Consequences

Second, tough love clarifies the consequences for unrepentant sin without trying to control the other person. When God first gave His bride the Promised Land, He clarified the terms of their marriage. He said, in effect, "If you are a faithful wife, you will enjoy prosperity and safety; if you are unfaithful, I will neither supply your needs nor protect you from harm" (Deut. 28). In other words, the marriage covenant established specific boundaries. He didn't attempt to manipulate or control His spouse; He merely communicated what behavior He would honor, and what sins He could not reward. As Henry Cloud and John Townsend explain,

> Our model is God. He does not really "set limits" on people to "make them" behave. God sets standards, but he lets people be who they are and then separates himself from them when they misbehave, saying in effect, "You can be that way if you choose, but you cannot come into my house." Heaven is a place for the repentant, and all are welcome.
>
> But God limits his exposure to evil, unrepentant people as should we. Scripture is full of admonitions to separate ourselves from people who act in destructive ways (Matt. 18:15–17; 1 Cor. 5:9–13). We are not being unloving. Separating ourselves protects love, because we are taking a stand against things that destroy love.[4]

The Lord's indictment of Israel's unfaithfulness included a reminder that He would no longer provide for her physical needs and continued safety (Hos. 2:6–13).

## Call for Repentance

Third, tough love calls for repentance without begging. The Lord explained the reason for His decision to divorce His wayward spouse, Israel:

> She will pursue her lovers, but she will not overtake them;
> And she will seek them, but will not find them.

Then she will say, "I will go back to my first husband,
For it was better for me then than now!" —Hosea 2:7

I will go away and return to My place
Until they acknowledge their guilt and seek My face;
In their affliction they will earnestly seek Me. —Hosea 5:15

God's purpose is always redemption. The goal of tough love is restoration, not retribution. Israel's persistent sin had erected a barrier to love that effectively ended the marriage. The Lord's writ of divorce included an invitation to restore their union on the sole condition of repentance. His invitation was earnest and heartfelt, but He never compromised His dignity.

Begging says, *Please come back to me; I can't live without you!* Dignity, on the other hand, declares, *When you have rejected your sin, I will be there to love and support you.* This is crucial when communicating with a partner whose perception of right and wrong, good and bad has been turned upside down by sin. Satan has convinced him or her that marriage is a trap while continued sin offers freedom.

## Offer a Plan for Reconciliation

Fourth, tough love offers a specific plan for reconciliation and the rebuilding of trust. Throughout the book of Hosea—indeed, throughout Israel's history—God called His unfaithful wife, Israel, to repentance. Close to the end of Hosea's oracle, the Lord explained in no uncertain terms what repentance and reconciliation would look like.

Return, O Israel, to the LORD your God,
For you have stumbled because of your iniquity.
Take words with you and return to the LORD.

Say to Him, "Take away all iniquity
And receive us graciously,
That we may present the fruit of our lips.
Assyria will not save us,
We will not ride on horses;
Nor will we say again, 'Our god,'
To the work of our hands;
For in You the orphan finds mercy." —Hosea 14:1–3

This is perhaps the most crucial element of redemptive divorce. A typical divorce decree declares the marriage dead and offers no hope of future reunion. Some spouses reconcile and marry each other again, but their cases are rare. At best, a typical divorce decree is a period at the end of a sad resignation; at worst, it is an exclamation point at the end of a bitter casting off of an unwanted partner.

Redemptive divorce involves two equally important documents, each charting a particular course. The divorce decree leads away from the marriage toward sin and describes in explicit detail the consequences that choice brings about. These consequences may include the loss of property, alimony and/or child support payments, and restricted access to the children (usually because of the normal division of time, but greater restriction may be necessary in cases where the dysfunction places them in danger). This official court document has a chilling effect, because it is a cold, dispassionate division of property all the way down to who keeps the flatware. It is also a callous division of the children's time between parents. Here is a small portion of an actual divorce decree:

Weekends—On weekends, beginning at the time the child's school is regularly dismissed on the first, third, and fifth Friday of each month and ending at the time the child's school resumes after the weekend.

Wednesdays—On Wednesday of each week during the regular school term, beginning at the time the child's school is regularly dismissed and ending at the time the child's school resumes on Thursday.

Christmas Holidays in Odd-Numbered Years—In odd-numbered years, beginning at the time the child's school is regularly dismissed on the day the child is dismissed from school for the Christmas school vacation and ending at noon on December 26.

Seeing the end of a marriage and the ripping apart of a family in such crisp, black-and-white detail just might be the jarring slap in the face a wayward partner needs.

The other document is the separation agreement. This legally binding contract includes many of the same provisions as the divorce decree, such as spousal support, child support, division of property, and child custody. The primary difference is the intent. Whereas the divorce decree leads away from the marriage, the separation agreement (as we will craft it) describes the means by which the wayward partner can restore the union and rebuild trust. (The next two chapters provide a description of the legal process and a guide to planning and preparing these documents.)

## Follow Through with Dependable Action

Fifth, tough love consistently follows through with dependable action. God illustrated the potential joy of restoration by giving Hosea's marriage a happy, new beginning. After an unknown period of time—perhaps years—Gomer's beauty faded. The aging harlot could no longer support her lifestyle on the gifts of her lovers, and she fell into debt. In that day and culture, people commonly sold themselves into slavery in order to meet their daily needs and to repay their creditors. With men no longer willing to pay her for sex, she had to choose between slavery and starvation. Sin's counterfeit freedom had led her into bondage. Then, the Lord directed Hosea to do something remarkable:

> Then the LORD said to me, "Go again, love a woman who is loved by her husband, yet an adulteress, even as the LORD loves the sons of Israel, though they turn to other gods and love raisin cakes." So I bought her for myself for fifteen shekels of silver and a homer and a half of barley. Then I said to her, "You shall stay with me for many days. You shall not play the harlot, nor shall you have a man; so I will also be toward you." —Hosea 3:1–3

Redemption. Grace that is truly amazing! Fifteen shekels was no small sum of money. David purchased a parcel of land with a threshing floor, complete with oxen, for just fifty shekels of silver (2 Sam. 24:24). Yet the silver required to purchase Gomer was half the traditional price of a slave. The addition of barley, the cheapest and coarsest grain, would not have made up the difference. In other words, Gomer had less value than a common slave, yet her husband purchased her freedom at great cost to himself, brought her home, and honored her as his wife.

By the end of Hosea's writings, the northern kingdom's divorce was final; but she had yet to hit bottom. Her lack of repentance forced the Lord's hand, and He had to follow through with the consequences He had promised. He predicted:

> They will not return to the land of Egypt;
> But Assyria—he will be their king

Because they refused to return to Me.
The sword will whirl against their cities,
And will demolish their gate bars
And consume them because of their counsels.
So My people are bent on turning from Me.
Though they call them to the One on high,
None at all exalts Him. —Hosea 11:5–7

Soon after Hosea's oracle, the Assyrian Empire began a series of invasions, finally wiping out the last of Israel in 722 BC. After deporting most of the inhabitants, Assyria transplanted people from other nations to Israel, encouraged intermarriage, and within a generation had successfully bred the remaining citizens out of existence. The southern kingdom of Judah was all that remained of the Hebrew people.

Consistent, dependable follow-through is absolutely essential to the success of redemptive divorce. Tough talk without tough action only compounds the negative implications of passivity. Furthermore, this discrepancy between words and deeds undermines dignity, which the wayward spouse must see in order to gain respect for his or her partner. If redemption is the goal, then the unrepentant partner must become convinced that the negative consequences are real. And that can only happen when a pledge promptly becomes reality.

## Who Has Control?

Nick's letter at the beginning of this chapter appeared to offer hope. After nearly a year of constant prayer and faithful waiting, his wife began to reconsider her choice. This crack in Joanne's resolve should have been reason for rejoicing. But Nick's letter is tinged with guilt rather than brimming with joy. His tentative response probably quashed the excitement of his family and friends, but he's wise to be cautious, although he may not understand why.

Nick's passive response allowed Joanne to wander in confusion far too long. As often happens, people want to have their sin without losing what sin destroys. Perhaps the most outrageous and perplexing example of this is when a man asks his wife to allow another woman into the marriage bed. In Joanne's case, she walked out of her marriage and deliberately left the door open. Then, when Nick "finally gave up" and moved to close the door, Joanne suddenly found salvation and said she "wants to work on our marriage." The grapevine suggested that Joanne would like to reconcile, yet she hasn't closed the door on her relationship with the other man!

No wonder Nick is confused and doesn't feel he can make a decision. The person least qualified and least capable of making competent life choices has all the control. As long as the wayward spouse has the power to determine the fate of the marriage, the end will come only after a long, heartrending process. And if reconciliation ever does occur, the prolonged period of sin only gives the upright partner more heartache to heal and makes granting trust much more difficult. Depending upon the circumstance and the nature of the unrepentant sin—such as adultery, which requires immediate action, or compulsive gambling, which is more ambiguous—the response should be prompt.

While redemptive divorce allows the upright partner to reclaim power for himself or herself, it is not an attempt to control or coerce the wayward partner. Redemptive divorce merely defines the sinner's options and clarifies the consequences of each, while demanding a choice sooner rather than later.

# Five

## Putting Divorce Proceedings into Perspective

*I am writing to you because my family and I need prayer. About four weeks ago, my husband assaulted me in front of our three children, after which I filed charges for domestic violence. The trial is still four months away, and until recently, I felt sure he would be convicted. However, he has filed a countersuit accusing me of abusing alcohol, alleging that I am mentally and emotionally unstable, and asked the court to declare me unfit to care for our children. While none of this is true, he was able to convince the judge—who has a reputation for siding with husbands—and was awarded custody of our children. The judge also declared that he can live at home while I find somewhere else to live. I also have to pay child support despite the fact he makes a six-figure income and I will be lucky to make minimum wage. I was a stay-at-home mom for our entire marriage.*

*Our youngest son has been diagnosed with hypoglycemia, which requires careful management of his diet as well as medication to help him fight his ear infections. But my husband isn't consistent, and our son is growing weaker and sicker as time goes by. Now our other two boys are beginning to suffer severe anxiety.*

*My only hope is to convince another judge to reverse this decision and gain custody of our sons, perhaps based on neglect. But my husband has changed all our bank accounts and cancelled our credit cards so that I can't even afford a place to live, much less the cost of an attorney. I don't even have enough to pay the child support I owe by the end of the month.*

*How could this happen? I'm not the one who beat and choked my partner. I'm not the one who's neglecting our children. He should be living on the street, yet I can't go into my own home without permission.*

*I have never felt so alone. I have never faced such injustice. I don't know what I'm going to do.*

*Eva*

Eva's tragedy is not uncommon. Earnest Christians desperately trying to resolve impossible situations frequently do everything possible to avoid the legal system, usually because they believe that seeking an attorney's help is somehow wrong. Unfortunately, the sinning spouse is all too willing to use any means necessary to retain control and to preserve his or her pattern of sin. Sooner or later, though, the matter nearly always lands before a judge, who typically hands the short end of justice to the least prepared spouse. And no one suffers more than the children.

This sadly common scenario can be avoided, but only if we dispel some common moral and legal myths surrounding divorce. Jesus commanded us to be "shrewd as serpents and innocent as doves" (Matt. 10:16). Therefore, let us understand the divorce process from a legal standpoint and then bring the entire matter under the authority of Scripture. That will be our purpose in this chapter.

## Common Myths About the Legal System and Divorce

No one loves a courtroom drama more than my wife. Her abiding love for truth and justice finds great satisfaction in seeing a team of lawyers uncover the facts, present them to a jury in open court, and ultimately prove their case. She's comforted to see each person— except the bad guy and his attorneys—play his or her part in a system designed to expose reality and place responsibility where it belongs. If only life were so pure.

In the interest of pursuing the truth, let's examine some common assumptions about the American system of justice and the divorce process.

### Myth #1: You Don't Need to Involve the Courts If You Just Do What Is Right

Eva thought if she simply did what was right, the courts would behave like a watchful parent and move to protect and support her. It's a common misconception. Those of us who do not have regular interaction with the judicial branch of our government tend to think of the court system as an entity—that is, a mission-focused agency of the government whose sole purpose is to fairly and impartially safeguard the rights of people, particularly the downtrodden and defenseless. While the American judicial system is perhaps the finest in the world, it is not an organization in this sense. It is, instead, a meeting ground, governed by rules, where people who disagree on the definition of right and wrong try to convince the government to take their side in a dispute. Therefore, the judicial system can be capable of accomplishing great good or perpetrating astounding evil, depending upon who's involved in a particular case.

Our system of laws and courts is neither good nor evil. We are much better to think of the judicial system as a powerful tool that can be utilized for either good or evil, depending upon who wields it. And in the hands of Eva's abusive husband, it became a weapon.

## Myth #2: Courts Care About Who Is at Fault in the Breakup of a Marriage and Will Favor the Innocent Party

At one time, courts would only grant a divorce when one party could prove the other to be at fault for the failure of the marriage. The grounds for divorce differed slightly in each state, but most recognized the obvious: infidelity, abandonment, abuse, or extreme neglect. Furthermore, the court would consider the severity of these grounds when awarding spousal support, child custody, and property to the innocent party.

Now, however, nearly every state recognizes what is called a *no-fault* divorce. This option allows one party to divorce the other without having to prove grounds or even gaining his or her consent. The court merely declares the marriage dissolved because at least one partner claims the union is irretrievably broken and beyond hope of reconciliation. At this point, the financial and practical matters of the divorce settlement depend on a number of other factors, such as how long the couple was married, the potential earning ability of each spouse, how much each partner contributed to the family's financial status, and who provided primary care for the children. No-fault also means that the state cannot be asked to enter a judgment dividing property unequally based on the shortcomings or the fault of either spouse. A settlement that divides property in such a way as to punish either spouse will not survive if challenged in court.

## Myth #3: Marriage Is a Sacred Matter in Which the Government Should Not Be Involved

The state will become involved in the institution of marriage only as we allow it. A couple submits to a small amount of government involvement when they obtain a marriage license before the wedding ceremony. This document merely informs the courts that two people are married and should be treated that way with respect to the law. Similarly, a parting couple must file for, and receive, a decree of divorce confirming that the state no longer recognizes them as married. All other matters concerning divorce or separation can be settled by one of several other means. The court has no other involvement unless the couple insists on fighting it out before a judge.

## Myth #4: Filing for Divorce Is an Unnecessary and Cruel Formality

In an ideal world, we could apply tough love without government involvement. However, people with this perspective typically underestimate the lengths to which a wayward spouse will go to defend his or her sinful choice and are frequently surprised to find themselves on the defendant's side of the courtroom. Because the legal system can become a dangerous weapon in the wrong hands, the upright partner must secure it or place it out of reach so the wayward partner has less opportunity to hurt someone.

Filing a petition or complaint for divorce with the court protects the upright spouse in several important ways. (Keep in mind that the petition can be rescinded at any time.)

*Legal Protection.* Simply packing up and leaving could constitute abandonment unless the upright spouse had to move out to preserve his or her own safety or the safety of the children. Even then, credible proof may be required later. In many states, the sinning spouse would have a strong case for a *fault* divorce. Furthermore, in some states, the person initiating the complaint gains the advantage of greater control over the agenda, timing, and tone of the entire divorce process. If the upright spouse does not use the legal system with wisdom, he or she could forfeit significant legal power or even become legally powerless despite how right he or she may be.

*Financial Protection.* Whatever physical and financial situation exists during separation commonly becomes the basis for the terms of the divorce. For instance, if the upright spouse vacates the home and, out of good conscience, provides one thousand dollars each month to cover bills, it will be almost impossible to convince the court that he or she should pay less after the divorce is final. The judge will also resist changing the existing living arrangements in order to preserve stability for the children.

Filing a petition and using the courts will provide structure for the financial arrangement from the very beginning.

*Physical Protection.* Temporary restraining orders are more easily obtained when they ask for reasonable protections in connection with a petition for divorce (the first official step in any divorce case). For instance, if the upright spouse is worried that his or her partner might become violent, disappear with the children, or deny access to bank funds or the family car, a temporary order can provide stability until the circumstances become less volatile.

## Myth #5: It's Morally Wrong to File for Divorce Because It "Separates what God Has Put Together"

As we discovered in chapter 2, a divorce decree doesn't end a marriage any more than a death certificate kills a person. Unrepentant sin renders a marriage null and void. The decree is merely a formal declaration in writing of what has already occurred in life. While filing for divorce and serving one's spouse with the papers is often an act of spiteful vengeance, it doesn't have to be. As we will discover, carefully constructed divorce papers can become the best—and perhaps last—great hope to revive a dead or dying marriage and to redeem a wayward partner.

## A Standard Divorce

The divorce process is relatively straightforward, at least in terms of the legal steps involved. Divorce cases become messy or complicated only because people make them that way. The path to dissolving a marriage requires no more than four steps.

### Step #1: File a Petition for Divorce

*Filing a petition* for divorce (also called a *complaint*) initiates the divorce process. A petition informs the court that one partner (known as the *petitioner*) is prepared to end his or her marriage to the other, declares the reason for the decision, and states the petitioner's preference for how the court should award custody, grant support, and divide property. Almost all of the fifty states recognize both types of petition: fault and no-fault.

A no-fault divorce essentially states that the couple cannot continue together because of irreconcilable differences, which is another way of saying it simply didn't work out. Many consider this a more civil means of ending the marriage, one that preserves the dignity of both partners by refusing to point fingers. While a no-fault petition appears to be more kind, it will not be effective if redeeming the wayward partner is the desired outcome.

A fault divorce requires the upright partner to state why the marriage should be declared dead by the court and to prove how his or her spouse killed it. Each state has its own list of recognized marriage-ending factors. Texas, for example, acknowledges the following grounds for divorce: cruelty, adultery, conviction of a felony, abandonment,[1] living apart for more than three years, and confinement to a mental hospital for at least three years for an incurable mental disorder. Depending upon the particular issue at hand, the upright spouse will have to work closely with an attorney to draft an effective petition that conforms to his or her state's guidelines.

## Step #2: Serve the Papers

*Serving the papers* officially notifies the other partner that a petition for divorce has been filed with the court and then establishes a certain amount of time during which he or she must respond. Each state has its own requirements for how the documents can be delivered, but most allow any one of four methods: hand delivery by the spouse, formal service by a sheriff or constable, a private process server, or registered mail.

## Step #3: File the Response

*Filing the response* (also known as *answering*) officially acknowledges receipt of the petition. The *respondent* (as he or she is known by the court) uses this document to indicate whether he or she disagrees with the grounds for divorce or plans to contest the terms of the settlement.

## Step #4: Issue the Divorce Decree

*Issuing the decree* concludes the entire matter in the eyes of the court. Once both partners agree on the language and terms of the petition, the court signs the document and it becomes a part of the state's public records. If the partners cannot agree on the terms, even after mediation, they can present their cases at trial and allow a judge to decide for them. Either way, once the court completes its part, the terms of the settlement are enforceable by law, and the two individuals are no longer recognized as a married couple.

## Legal Separation

A common alternative to divorce will be important for our purposes as we offer the wayward spouse a responsible means of restoring the marriage upon repentance. Many states sanction some form of legal separation. Those states that don't, usually recognize postnuptial agreements, which can accomplish the same objective.

A legal separation functions as a divorce in every respect with the sole exception that the two individuals are considered a married couple and will be treated as such under the law. The terms of the agreement—including grounds for parting, custody arrangements, provision of spousal and/or child support, and division of property—are legally binding on each partner once accepted by the court, and the agreement can remain in place indefinitely. This separation agreement can also include other provisions, such as required counseling, participation in a rehabilitation program, and periodic testing or evaluation by a third party.

## The Redemptive Divorce Process

Redemptive divorce seeks to give a redeeming purpose to the divorce process. Instead of using the documents and procedures of civil court to officially dissolve a marriage, redemptive divorce employs them to give the wayward spouse an incentive to work for restoration. Therefore, redemptive divorce is a tough-love confrontation patterned after the method of godly confrontation described by Jesus in Matthew 18:15–17. After describing God as a faithful shepherd who leaves the ninety-nine to search for one straying sheep, He instructed His disciples:

> If your brother sins, go and show him his fault in private; if he listens to you, you have won your brother. But if he does not listen to you, take one or two more with you, so that by the mouth of two or three witnesses every fact may be confirmed. If he refuses to listen to them, tell it to the church; and if he refuses to listen even to the church, let him be to you as a Gentile and a tax collector. —Matthew 18:15–17

The sole purpose of confrontation is redemption. Redemption restores the relationship between the two people involved; however, refusal to repent leads to consequences. To be treated as a Gentile and a tax collector was not to be mistreated or reviled but merely to be removed as a damaging influence and then regarded as an evangelistic prospect rather than a fellow believer with whom to commune.[2] When an upright church faithfully follows this pattern of church discipline, a simple and clear choice is presented to the unrepentant member: *turn your back on this sin and make it right, or we cannot in good conscience allow you to remain a part of our fellowship of genuine believers.* Similarly, redemptive divorce presents the wayward partner with a choice between two alternatives: outright divorce or a structured separation with the possibility of reconciliation.

Ideally, the Matthew 18:15–17 pattern for godly confrontation accomplishes three important objectives. First, it describes the offense in sufficient detail as to be clear and offers enough evidence as to be irrefutable. Second, it offers the wayward brother an opportunity to repent of sin, reconcile the estrangement, and restore the relationship. And third, it clarifies the consequences for refusing the offer of reconciliation. Redemptive divorce employs two legal documents to confront a spouse who stubbornly refuses to let go of his or her sin: a final decree of divorce and a separation agreement.

At this point, trying to describe these legal documents in detail creates a dilemma. Any description must contain sufficient detail to be useful, at least for the purposes of illustration. However, the laws and procedures in each of the fifty states differ significantly enough to make any description inaccurate. Furthermore, I am not an attorney, so any information you gain from this book, while thoroughly researched and written in good faith, cannot be considered legal counsel. *Do nothing without competent legal counsel from someone qualified to guide you in your particular state.*

Because I am most familiar with the current laws of the state of Texas, I will describe these two documents according to present standards in Texas and demonstrate how someone there could use them. The specifics are not as important as the main ideas. Observe the details as a means of gleaning the principles, and then work with a competent attorney in your state to put them into practice.

## The Original Petition and Decree of Divorce

The petitioner's legal representative prepares the original petition for divorce, which will serve as the basis for the final decree. The petitioner's representative will also draft a final decree of divorce, which becomes the working document for negotiation with the other partner. Both the original petition and the final decree declare the grounds for divorce.

While the reasons for the breakdown of the marriage must conform to the particular state's guidelines, the petitioner has a fair amount of latitude in describing the situation. Excessive detail is neither desired nor helpful; however, the grounds should satisfactorily answer two questions:

1. Why has continuing to live together become impossible?
2. Why is the marriage beyond any reasonable hope of restoration?

The decree should describe the wayward partner's unrepentant sin as the grounds for divorce, and these grounds must be supported by evidence that will satisfy a judge. The language used to allege *insupportability* (why the union has become hopelessly broken) is crucial to the redemptive divorce process. It declares in explicit terms that the reason for the breakdown of the marriage is not the wayward spouse's sin, per se, but his or her refusal to repent.

Here is a very brief example taken from an actual divorce decree in Texas:

THE PARTIES AGREE AND THE COURT FINDS that this divorce was not the desire of JOHN JAMES DOE and, despite the existence of fault on the part of MARY MAE DOE in the breakup of the marriage, JOHN JAMES DOE remained desirous of reconciliation. The sole reason the parties have agreed that there is no reasonable expectation of reconciliation is due to MARY MAE

DOE's unwillingness to reconcile. Therefore, THE COURT FINDS that there is no reasonable expectation of reconciliation in this case.

IT IS THEREFORE ORDERED AND DECREED that JOHN JAMES DOE, Petitioner, is granted a divorce from MARY MAE DOE, Respondent, and the marriage between them is dissolved on the grounds of adultery and abandonment.

Note that both crucial questions have been answered. The grounds for divorce are adultery and abandonment. But, more importantly, the reason the marriage remains hopeless is Mary Mae Doe's refusal to stop the behavior that makes living together impossible. This second statement is vital to the redemptive divorce process because it points to the primary issue at hand. The language should be carefully crafted so that the decree of divorce says, in effect, "This piece of paper merely confirms in writing that my spouse has rejected marriage to me in favor of his or her sin."

Besides satisfying several technical requirements of the court, the remainder of the document addresses every practical matter involved in dividing one life into two, including child custody and visitation, spousal and child support, and division of property and debts. States that have adopted a no-fault approach to divorce will not allow the terms of a settlement to be punitive, so money and access to the children cannot become incentives to reconcile. While this might become a strong temptation, coersion is not the aim of redemptive divorce.

Redemptive divorce is a tough-love expression of grace. And grace is costly. Victory in this case should not be defined by how much *stuff* the upright partner is able to win in court. Victory is reclaiming the power to shape one's own future apart from the dysfunction of a wayward mate and the ability to maintain a peaceful home without the constant drama and chaos created by unrepentant sin. And this victory may require sacrificing material wealth or financial security. Nevertheless, the upright spouse and his or her attorney should be as aggressive as possible, not to punish, control, or coerce the wayward spouse but to minimize the negative impact on the innocent parties affected by the divorce.

We don't want the potential loss of material wealth to become an undue influence. The multifaceted loss through divorce will be incentive enough to reconcile without making it worse. Besides, a decision to repent and work toward restoration of the marriage made under duress would be pointless. Realistically, the wayward spouse may elect to reconcile simply to minimize his or her own loss, which is not ideal, but it's a beginning. Then, once the spell of sin begins to lift, we hope he or she will fight for the marriage because it is right. Any other motive will quickly fade.

Essentially, the final decree of divorce, if signed, represents the choice of the wayward partner to abandon his or her spouse for the sake of continued sin. Should the confrontation go this route, the wayward spouse will likely contest terms of the decree. In this case, the upright spouse may be required to concede some matters of importance; however, this should come only after a fight and must never include changing the language concerning grounds and insupportability. In other words, fight hard and refuse to call the divorce anything but what it truly is: abandonment of the marriage in favor of sin.

## The Separation Agreement

A separation agreement is a contract that binds married partners to a set of terms. Whereas the terms of a divorce settlement can be decided by a judge if the parties fail to reach an agreement, this postnuptial contract is entirely voluntary. In many states, a separation agreement can be court-ordered, which gives the upright spouse some extra leverage; however, the spirit of redemptive divorce would favor a softer approach when negotiating a separation agreement. This is, after all, the option we hope the wayward partner will choose. Nevertheless, the actual provisions for child custody, spousal and/or child support, property division, and so on should be identical to the divorce decree, except where the wayward partner's sin impacts the safety and welfare of the children.

In states where postnuptial and separation agreements tend to be vulnerable when challenged, a creative attorney will have to find the most appropriate means of accomplishing two important objectives. First, the separation agreement must stabilize the living arrangements and assure adequate provision for everyone in the family during the time the couple lives apart. Second, it must allow for either future reconciliation or divorce at the discretion of either partner.

Ideally, in addition to providing for the physical needs of the upright spouse and the children, the separation agreement will include detailed provisions for the rebuilding of trust and, ultimately, restoration of the marriage. For example, for a man who left his wife to live with another woman, the separation agreement could stipulate:

- The man must end his relationship with the woman, move out, and eliminate all contact with her.

- The man must not engage in a romantic or sexual relationship with any other person.

- The man must participate in individual counseling and accountability with a Christian counselor at least once a week.

- When his counselor deems it appropriate and by mutual consent, couples' counseling may replace individual counseling.

## Time to Heal

The decree of divorce and the separation agreement represent two alternatives. Choosing to sign or negotiate the terms in the divorce decree is essentially a choice for sin over the marriage, whereas the separation agreement is the exact opposite. The separation agreement then becomes the means by which the wayward spouse can officially declare his or her intent to turn from the behavior that has destroyed the marriage and begin to restore the union. So why is a contract necessary for this? Why can't the wayward partner simply repent and begin to do what is right? Carrie's letter illustrates the reason:

*When I married my husband, I married my dream man. I had no doubt that our marriage would be a lifelong fairytale. I just knew our love was strong and true. My fairytale turned out to be a nightmare. After the birth of our first child, he turned to methamphetamines, and our lives spiraled out of control. Work, marriage, and children proved to be too much for him. We almost lost everything to his addiction. By God's grace and with the help of supportive friends and family, he broke his habit. But he eventually started using again and then had an affair, which almost killed me.*

*My husband has again broken his habit, this time for good, and he's given his life to Christ. He wants to recommit to our marriage and promises to become a better father. And I believe it's real. I really want to forgive him, but the pain is almost more than I can bear. Every wedding promise, every little girl's dream, every expectation has been shattered along with my trust. After the lies, the infidelity, emotional abuse, and false accusations, I feel completely used up and totally worthless.*

*I thank God that my husband has finally repented and wants to do what is right, but I stopped caring a long time ago. As terrible as it sounds, I don't want him near me anymore. I don't want to feel this way, and I have begged God to help me, but I don't feel like He hears my cries. I searched myself and asked the Lord to take away any barriers to His healing. But I just don't understand why He has allowed me to be hurt so much.*

*Sometimes I feel like God loves my husband more than He loves me. I was wounded so deeply, yet I must forgive while my husband gets away with causing so much harm. I know this isn't the right way to see it, so I keep looking to Christ to help me forgive and overcome all of this.*

*Please continue to pray for me and my family.*

Carrie

Forgiveness is not a feeling. We tend to think of forgiveness as the ability to have a relationship with our offender without feeling angry, sorrowful, fearful, resentful, or any other negative emotion. In other words, we tend to confuse forgiveness with healing or the ability to trust. Forgiveness is a lot of things, but it is not a feeling. Forgiveness is a choice, something we decide to do.

While the choice to forgive is uncomplicated—either let the other person off the hook or continue to hold him accountable—it is anything but easy. In the words of Neil Anderson,

Forgiveness is agreeing to live with the consequences of another person's sin. Forgiveness is costly; we pay the price of the evil we forgive. Yet you're going to live with those consequences whether you want to or not; your only choice is whether you will do so in the bitterness of unforgiveness or the freedom of forgiveness. That's how Jesus forgave you—He took the consequences of your sin upon Himself. All true forgiveness is substitutional, because no one really forgives without bearing the penalty of the other person's sin.[3]

Carrie has genuinely chosen to forgive her repentant husband. She has made the difficult choice to live with the consequences of his sin without seeking revenge or requiring him to suffer as she had. Yet she still suffers the pangs of rejection and struggles to put away resentment—even toward God. Carrie doesn't lack forgiveness. She needs healing. And she needs her husband to earn her trust again. The relationship must be rebuilt from the rubble that once was her marriage, starting with a brand-new foundation.

According to Drs. Cloud and Townsend, the process of healing and restoration has three interrelated yet distinct stages:

1. *Forgiveness has to do with the past.* Forgiveness is not holding something someone has done against her. It is letting go. It only takes one to offer forgiveness. And just as God has offered forgiveness to everyone, we are expected to do the same —Matthew 6:12; 18:35.

2. *Reconciliation has to do with the present.* It occurs when the other person apologizes and accepts forgiveness. It takes two to reconcile.

3. *Trust has to do with the future.* It deals with both what you will risk happening again and what you will open yourself up to. A person must show through his actions that he is trustworthy before you trust him again —Matt. 3:8; Prov. 4:23.[4]

Time will eventually heal Carrie's wounds. The amount of time will depend upon what kind of guidance she receives and how safe she is from further injury. Like physical wounds, emotional wounds require careful attention and a protected environment if they are to heal properly. A sound separation agreement must allow adequate time apart so that the upright partner has time to heal in safety, the offending partner has an opportunity to address whatever personal issues led to his or her sin, and the couple can allow trust to rebuild slowly and responsibly.

During the separation, each partner must work individually and as a couple to prepare for the time they can reunite. To deal adequately with the past, Dave Carder, an experienced family counselor and best-selling author, would encourage Carrie to communicate what she needs to hear from her husband. He would also have her husband make a list of his offenses and rank them in the order of least to worst. Then, he would have Carrie's husband begin confessing and apologizing for each offense. Carrie's husband must understand the internal forces that contributed to his making the choices he did and learn how to manage them differently. Carrie, for her part, must learn how to express the depth of her sorrow in terms her husband can understand and to communicate what behavior will allow her to extend trust to her husband again. She must also discover and own her contribution to the breakdown of the marriage. This is sometimes a controversial notion, but it is crucial to rebuilding, especially after infidelity. Carder's book, *Torn Asunder: Recovering from Extramarital Affairs,* is the best resource I know for couples healing from this kind of devastation. And the principles are very helpful for couples challenged to overcome any breach in trust.[5]

> Forgiveness is a lot of things, but it is not a feeling. Forgiveness is a choice, something we decide to do.

Restoration will not be easy for anyone. The upright partner must open himself or herself to the possibility of reinjury. The repentant partner must endure the excruciating process of self-examination and reformation. The rebuilding of the marriage will be fraught with danger and marked by setbacks. And, truth be told, few couples make it. Nevertheless, redemption is possible, not only for individuals but for couples. Given the right environment and expert guidance, God can raise a temple of extraordinary grace from the ashes of sin. But it won't happen automatically. Reconciliation and restoration must be intentional. Redemption requires tough love backed by consequences and actions that have genuine impact.

> Given the right environment and expert guidance, God can raise a temple of extraordinary grace from the ashes of sin.

Redemptive divorce is not a game of bluffing and brinksmanship. Neither is it an attempt to control or coerce the wayward partner to behave a certain way. This act of severe mercy merely states the truth as it is—the marriage is over—and reduces the future to two alternative paths, each having its own consequences. The involvement of lawyers and the looming authority of the civil courts merely make those consequences real to a person under the deluding spell of sin.

While redemptive divorce depends upon the expert preparation and execution of legal documents, it is much more. Redemptive divorce is a process that requires committed teamwork, specific goals, and careful planning.

# Six

## A Team, a Goal, and a Plan

*Our marriage of twelve years was full of abundant blessings: four children, successful careers, health, roles in church leadership, Bible studies, and Christian fellowship. We often spoke of our abundance and would quickly give God the glory. So when James told me he was in an "inappropriate relationship," it came as a total shock. There really are no words to capture the ensuing wave of horror and despair that flooded over me. Our life as I knew it was over. The man I thought I married was gone, and in his place stood a stranger. At one point in my journal I wrote, "Can a broken vase be made new again? Not broken, but shattered? Won't there always be a weak place open for repeated attack? Lord, are we fixable?"*

*When James decided to fully repent, a miracle took place. The man who was so entangled with pride, selfishness, and lust disappeared. In his place was a naked, shaken child who understood that God would never leave him or forsake him even though he could not say the same for himself. He surrendered everything at the cross. There wasn't a single thing he withheld. He was transformed.*

*Today, six years later, our marriage is like nothing we had ever dreamed possible. We are so much more open and honest with each other—it starts with being open and honest with God. Our personal devotions and couple's devotions are routine aspects of our lives. We vividly understand the depth to which we can be deceived when we are not actively protecting ourselves by putting on the full armor of God. We are also sharing the story with others that they might benefit from our mistakes and lessons learned.*

*The lessons that we have learned and the level of intimacy that we now experience within our marriage and our walks with God most definitely leave me having no regrets. I didn't know how He would do it, but He did. Are we fixable? "All things are possible with God" —Mark 10:27.*

*Mary Ann*

The confrontation is a crucial event. It is, in many respects, a moment of truth for the unrepentant spouse. He will hear his sin named. He will come face-to-face with the destruction it has brought upon the people he loves. The wayward spouse will recognize that his choices will determine the future of everyone with a stake in the marriage—the once-united partners, their children, their extended family, even their church and community. It is the apex of the redemptive process, the culmination of meticulous planning, a time that marks the end of the status quo and the beginning of new life for the upright spouse and, hopefully, a turning point for the marriage.

The purpose of redemptive divorce is not to coerce or control the unrepentant spouse; it is merely to clarify three important facts. First, the wayward spouse has the power to decide the future of the marriage. Second, the upright spouse wants the marriage to continue and remains committed to restoring the union. Third, a refusal to turn away from the behavior that has destroyed the marriage will lead to divorce, while repentance will lead to complete restoration. Because a moment like this holds such potential for either blessing or harm for everyone involved, nothing must be left to chance. This tough-love confrontation requires careful planning, which includes setting short-term and long-term goals, deciding what course of action would most please the Lord based on the particular challenges to the marriage, gathering important documentation, and coordinating the help of experts.

This sounds like a tall order, especially to someone emotionally worn down by the stress of a dysfunctional marriage. But, as they say, Rome wasn't built in a day. Preparation will require several weeks and can be broken down into manageable tasks. When taken in order and completed thoroughly, these steps will lead to a tough-love conversation that may or may not become the catalyst for restoration but will certainly bring relief to the upright spouse.

## Help for the Weary

Unfortunately, a marriage torn apart by sin typically leaves the upright partner drained of energy and aching for hope. He or she needs the help of a small team of people who understands the process and will remain committed to seeing it through to completion. Success depends upon the coordinated efforts of three people in addition to the upright spouse.

### Family Law Attorney

A family law attorney, preferably Christian, will be needed to guide the upright spouse through the legal process of divorce. Each case and each jurisdiction has their own peculiarities, and because redemptive divorce is a new concept, a do-it-yourself divorce kit will not suffice. A competent attorney will not only understand the laws of a particular state but also be familiar with certain judges and how they decide cases. Moreover, he will know how to use the instruments and procedures of the court to accomplish the specific goals of the upright spouse and achieve the objective of redemptive divorce.

Once the upright partner has made the decision to take a strong stand against continued sin, impatience has a tendency to pull him or her forward. At first, every attorney looks like a hero, but great care must be taken. The choice of counsel will be crucial. Any attorney can begin a case well, but only the best know how to achieve their clients' goals when things don't go exactly as planned.

Lawyers used to be known as *advocates*. An advocate advises and represents. Many offer lots of competent advice, but few do a good job representing their clients. Most have the ability to map out an effective legal strategy, but few respond quickly and nimbly when the opposing side pulls an unexpected trick. Just like any other profession, some lawyers are conscientious, take time to understand their clients' needs, and are willing to take a creative approach to solving problems. Others are in it for the paycheck and will do little more than the minimum to clear a case and maximize their billable hours. Some have fill-in-the-blank documents they have refined over the years and are reluctant to do anything beyond the tried-and-true methods that have served them well. Others approach each case as a unique challenge to their abilities and attack it with creativity and gusto.

Finding the right attorney will be a painstaking part of the process. At the very least, the attorney must have proper credentials along with significant experience in family law. Redemptive divorce will require more. The right attorney must also possess rare qualities. This attorney must be someone who understands and supports the goals of the upright spouse and, just as importantly, someone willing to be creative to achieve them. While this approach to divorce and reconciliation is admittedly a radical departure from the norm, none of the documents or the concepts is foreign to the courts. Nevertheless, the attorney must be courageous and committed.

## Christian Counselor

A licensed, professional Christian counselor, preferably one who has experience conducting an intervention, provides spiritual and emotional guidance along the way and then helps the upright spouse confront his or her partner once the planning is complete and everything is in place. Throughout the planning process, the suffering partner will need help establishing boundaries, processing emotions, caring for the emotional needs of his or her children, and remaining faithful to the ultimate objective: redemption of the marriage.

During planning, the counselor will work with the upright spouse to define what "restoration of the marriage" means in a practical sense. In other words, what would have to happen for the upright spouse to feel secure living as husband and wife again, and what must each of the partners do to make this possible? The counselor will prepare the upright spouse for the confrontation and facilitate the discussion at that meeting. This will be particularly effective if the counselor has already established a rapport with the offending spouse. The word *divorce* will undoubtedly drown out the word *redemption*, so a trusted third party will be essential.

## Accountability Partner

An accountability partner provides emotional support and helps coordinate many of the logistical needs of the upright spouse. He will arrange childcare during meetings, help prepare living arrangements should the upright spouse have to move away from home, store important documents or valuables, and even offer moral support during court hearings or other legal proceedings. The upright spouse will also need lots of encouragement when emotions occasionally take over. This faithful friend will not only offer steady counsel during turbulent times but also may need to enlist the help of several people to bear the enormous emotional load.

The accountability partner should be a strong, stable person of the same gender as the upright spouse and preferably from outside the family.

## Preparing for the Future

The redemptive divorce process can be divided into four stages: homework, preparation, confrontation, and follow-through.

### Homework

Before contacting an attorney and wading into a sea of legal details, before doing anything concrete, the upright spouse must prepare. This includes setting short-term and long-term goals, deciding what course of action would most please the Lord based on the particular challenges to the marriage, and gathering important documentation. This stage of the process will feel like a waste of time because nothing seems to be happening while the destructive behavior continues, but it is in fact the most important. Failing to complete this phase is like starting a long road trip without a map. You can ask for directions along the way and eventually get where you're going, but how much time, energy, and money will you have wasted?

Legal advocates want clients who are organized and motivated with clearly defined goals. Good planning will be detailed, but it doesn't have to be complicated. Several worksheets at the end of this book will help the upright spouse think through many of the most important issues. The worksheets include:

- Preparing to Live Apart
- Monthly Household Expenses
- Documents Checklist
- Preparing to Respond
- Priorities for Negotiating the Settlement

I urge the upright spouse to be patient and to give considerable thought to these forms. He or she should answer the questions thoroughly, focus on facts more than feelings, and diligently gather all of the documents listed. This information will be required eventually, and the whole process will be much less taxing later if these details are addressed at the beginning. A competent Christian counselor would be an invaluable resource during this time. If the upright spouse doesn't already have the support of a counselor, he or she should enlist the help of one while completing the homework phase. The same is true of an accountability partner.

*Short-Term Goals (Separation).* Confronting the wayward spouse officially begins a period of separation, at least for a short time. The responses to the questions on the worksheet "Preparing to Live Apart" will help an attorney prepare the necessary documents for a structured separation. The primary issues include:

1. *Shelter.* Where will the upright spouse and the children live while the couple is separated? If the upright spouse hopes to remain in the home long term, he or she should plan to stay at a hotel, the home of a loved one, or another safe location for the first few days but not more than a week. This will allow time for cooling off and provide the wayward spouse time to arrange another place to live. Then the long-term living arrangements must provide stability for several months,

perhaps even permanently if the wayward spouse ultimately chooses continued sin over the marriage. However, don't forget that a judge will be reluctant to change the living arrangements during separation when finalizing a divorce.

2. *Security.* How will the financial needs of the upright spouse and the children be met during separation? This will include daily living expenses as well as continued health care and debt repayment. If spousal and child support are requested, the monthly amount should be reasonable but generous. After all, separation is the result of the wayward spouse's stubborn refusal to put an end to behavior that has made cohabitation impossible. There is no reason the upright spouse should suffer more than he or she already has. Nevertheless, the proposed figure must be supported by facts. The worksheet "Monthly Household Expenses" will help estimate a reasonable monthly allotment, especially if the figures are based upon an average of the actual expenses for the previous six to twelve months.

In addition to the estimated expenses, the upright spouse should research every means possible of obtaining income, including public assistance, charity, or extra work, should the court not award support. Some states, such as Texas, are notoriously stingy when it comes to spousal support, even when it's temporary. So this might become an actual plan of action. Furthermore, the attorney will use this information to demonstrate a genuine need for support, so it must show an honest effort to explore every means of self-sufficiency.

3. *Stability.* How will the new living and financial arrangements provide greater *practical* stability for the children and the upright spouse than continued cohabitation? Some cases will be stronger than others, depending upon the marital issue involved. For instance, the constant chaos and household disruption caused by substance abuse may make holding down a job very difficult for the upright spouse

or may present such a distraction for the children that they cannot complete homework assignments.

Major issues should be stated first, described as briefly as possible, and focused on facts. A judge will usually skim over emotional appeals and will look for facts that can be supported by evidence, such as police reports, pictures, recordings, affidavits from witnesses, notes from teachers, report cards—anything that would convince a skeptic.

4. *Sanity.* How will the new living and financial arrangements provide greater emotional stability for the children and the upright spouse? The licensed, professional Christian counselor can help answer this question, preferably in writing on his or her official stationery. School counselors and teachers may be able to provide opinions about the effect of the present situation on the children, which will hopefully add credibility to the reason for separation.

*Necessary and Helpful Documents.* The attorney will also need several documents in order to devise an effective legal strategy and to prepare drafts of a divorce decree and a separation agreement that will pass legal muster. The upright spouse should make copies of the records listed on the "Documents Checklist," place them in a folder, and keep them in a secure place. Photocopies of legal documents will suffice in the short term, but official copies should be obtained as soon as possible.

This can be tedious and sometimes frustrating work, but it will pay great dividends throughout the process.

*Long-Term Goals (Divorce or Restoration).* It is important to note that the wayward spouse cannot be compelled to do anything—not morally and not legally. The upright spouse can only define the behavior he or she will allow in his or her presence and then respond to the choices of the wayward spouse accordingly. For instance, a wife cannot compel or even demand that her alcoholic husband stop drinking alcohol. However, she can decide where and with whom to live based upon his choice of behavior. In other words, the message of redemptive divorce is not, "Stop it, or else . . .", but "I love you, and I want to live with you, but my future cannot include your destructive behavior."

While separation is clearly the choice of the upright spouse, the fate of the marriage will be placed in the hands of the wayward spouse at the time of confrontation. What he or she will choose to do cannot be foreseen. All we can do is reduce the range of options to two—divorce or restoration—and then prepare to respond accordingly. The worksheet "Preparing to Respond" will help the upright spouse identify the specific issues that have placed the marriage in jeopardy and what circumstances would allow him or her to feel secure in restoring the union. This will help the attorney understand the long-term goals of the upright spouse and then prepare the two documents to achieve them.

Again, the terms of the divorce decree and the separation agreement cannot be punitive. Many states still allow for fault divorces; nevertheless, unequal division of property based on marital fault will render an agreement unenforceable. Therefore the terms of the decree and the separation agreement must conform to local standards, and they must be identical in each document. The primary difference between the two documents will be the intent: either dissolution of the marriage or its restoration.

Terms of divorce in a no-fault state are usually negotiated unless the parties cannot agree, in which case the courts will decide. Therefore, an attorney will work hard to propose terms that are likely to satisfy a judge. This doesn't mean that everything has to be split fifty-fifty, but it should avoid any appearance that one partner is trying to take advantage of the other.

The attorney must understand his or her client's priorities when preparing the initial draft of the settlement. Which issues are non-negotiable, which are important, and which can be used for bargaining? The worksheet "Priorities for Negotiating the Settlement" lists many of the major items commonly addressed. The upright spouse can use this form to guide the attorney.

As the upright spouse considers his or her priorities, the temptation will be to allow anger or resentment to take over. Here is where the Christian counselor and accountability partner can help the upright spouse keep a level head and focus on what's really important. Non-negotiable issues must be kept to a minimum and, where possible, supported by credible evidence. For example, if the upright spouse places a high priority on the issue of supervised visitation, he or she must have good reason to suspect that the safety of the children would be compromised without supervision and then offer credible evidence to support his or her fear. Moreover, the upright spouse should balance a strong stand on one issue by surrendering others, such as money or possessions.

Once the homework has been thoroughly completed and all documentation gathered, the upright spouse must then prepare for the day of confrontation and for life on his or her own thereafter.

## Preparation

Preparing for the day of confrontation must be done with utmost discretion, which may feel like sneaking around. And in many respects, it is. But the purpose for discretion is not to take advantage of the wayward spouse. On the contrary, it is to safeguard the best interest of everyone involved. The upright spouse must be able to confront his or her sinning partner from a position of strength, safe from retaliation or control. Ideally, during the confrontation and thereafter, the wayward partner will have no recourse but to face the matter at hand: his or her need to repent and the gracious offer of restoration.

Because separation commences immediately after confronting the wayward spouse, everything must be arranged in advance, including living arrangements, financial provisions, legal documents, and prearranged responses to every action the wayward spouse is likely to take. This begins with the upright partner establishing some measure of independence, even before selecting an attorney, including the following provisions.

*Independent Bank Accounts.* Some may not respond well to hearing the word *divorce* and may try to seize control of the couple's shared assets, including money in joint bank accounts. Prior to the confrontation, the upright spouse should establish new accounts in his or her name and preferably with a separate institution. He or she should deposit only funds that would not be missed until the day of confrontation. Then just prior to meeting, some of the funds, but not more than half, should be moved to the new accounts.

*Post Office Box.* Preparing for the confrontation will necessarily involve sending and receiving sensitive correspondence, including bank statements, bills, and legal information. Anything associated with plans for separation should be directed to a post office box.

*Duplicate Keys for House and Cars.* Traumatic events send some people into an emotional tailspin, and they try to restore order to their worlds by seizing control of whatever they can. The wayward spouse may try to prevent access to the home or cars, so having duplicate keys stored in a safe location might be a good idea.

*Safe-Deposit Box (or Other Secure Storage).* Valuable belongings, such as jewelry, mementos, spare keys, and copies of important documents, should be stored in a safe location somewhere other than the home. The home of a trusted friend or the accountability partner would suffice, but a safe-deposit box with the bank would allow easier access and would be more private.

*Prepaid Cell Phone for Secure Communication.* All communication with the attorney or anyone else associated with the separation should be done on a phone other than one shared by members of the family. Prepaid cell phones are inexpensive, easy to obtain, and offer greater security and privacy than phones shared by others in the family. Billing for the home phone and for cell phones typically includes a detailed accounting of every telephone number that calls in or out.

*Consultation with an Attorney.* The upright spouse should consult a competent family law attorney only after the other provisions have been established.

Most attorneys offer a free initial consultation to hear and consider the needs of a potential client. The upright spouse should be prepared to leave copies of the worksheet responses and the supporting documentation. At this meeting, the attorney will want to know the reason for taking legal action and what specific goals are to be accomplished. Having documents in hand will be very reassuring to the attorney, but he is unlikely to be familiar with redemptive divorce; therefore, some explanation will be necessary. Certainly, having a copy of this book might be helpful, but he can't be expected to read it. If the attorney seems initially closed to the idea, especially without taking time to understand it, then he is probably not the right person for the job.

Once the best attorney for the case has been retained, he must prepare the petition for divorce, a separation agreement, a decree of divorce, and any temporary orders that might be necessary. Much of the information the attorney needs will come from the worksheets and documents prepared in advance; however, several meetings may be required in order to work out a detailed strategy. Together, the upright spouse and the attorney must consider every potential action by the wayward spouse and formulate a response, not to dominate or coerce but to protect the upright spouse from retaliation or control.

While the divorce settlement will be reasonably straightforward, the separation agreement will be more complex. If possible, the path to restoration should be made part of the agreement with potential reconciliation left open to the mutual consent of the partners. Conversely, the decision to divorce must also remain an option for both partners.

The purpose of the separation agreement is not to force the wayward spouse to change his or her behavior or to seek professional help for problems. Naturally, this is our hope, and we want to make the path to restoration and healing an attractive option. But this cannot be the focus of the document. The purpose of the separation agreement is to provide structure to the separation during the process of rebuilding trust and to clearly communicate what the upright spouse desires.

Again, our purpose is not to coerce or control the wayward spouse. We merely want to offer the choice either to accept the divorce (thus admitting that he or she prefers continued sin to the marriage) or to accept a structured separation as a means of restoring the union.

## Confrontation

Once the legal documents have been prepared and the logistics of separation are in place, the wayward spouse must be confronted. A day or two before the scheduled meeting, the attorney must file the petition for divorce with the court and then notify the upright spouse. The wayward spouse should be called to meet in a neutral location—preferably in the office of the Christian counselor—where the upright spouse will be waiting. If the upright spouse plans to stay at a hotel or some other location during a cooling off period, bags should be packed and the children prepared to go there instead of home.

The counselor should moderate the meeting while saying as little as possible. After opening with prayer, he should state that the upright partner has something important to say and then remain quietly supportive. Because the upright spouse will undoubtedly experience intense nervousness, the tough-love confrontation should be written in advance, read aloud, and then provided as a cover letter for the divorce settlement and the separation agreement. And because the wayward spouse will certainly experience a broad range of powerful emotions, he or she will need to review the message later.

Two words must characterize the confrontation: *compassion* and *clarity*. The letter should cover four essential points: an affirmation of love, a description of behavior destructive to the marriage, a description of action taken by the upright spouse, and an appeal for repentance. The following sample letter illustrates the spirit of the confrontation and may help the upright spouse craft one of his or her own:

*My precious wife, Alice,*

*I love you more than mere words can express, and I desire nothing more than to remain your husband and to grow old with you. Today, I* am just as committed to our marriage vows as when I first spoke them thirteen years ago. However, your choices and continued behavior have made it very clear that you do not want this marriage.

You have repeatedly consumed alcohol to the point of intoxication and, each time, verbally and emotionally abused our children. You have been guilty of driving under the influence of alcohol on at least two occasions. (Copies of the police reports are attached.) You frequently drink too much in public, embarrass me with your obnoxious behavior, and then expect me to take care of you as you vomit through the night. You have been reprimanded by your employer for keeping a container of alcohol hidden at work and for smelling of liquor after lunch. (An affidavit from your boss is attached.) The doctor believes that alcohol abuse has caused your ulcers and predicts that your health will continue to decline as long as you continue to drink. (A letter from Dr. Smith is attached.) We have discussed your overuse of alcohol many times. We have sought counseling. You have been confronted by me, your family, and even our pastor, yet you refuse to seek help.

I cannot fully describe the damage your drinking has done to our marriage, our family, our household, and even our finances. The children do not have a mother because you are not able to care for them much of the time. They do not have a father because much of my energy is consumed by the chaos you create. The emotional damage to our family will require years of individual counseling, and I fear the harm to our children may be permanent. And between the money you spend on alcohol and the lost wages, we are slowly but surely going into debt.

I cannot keep you from abusing alcohol, but I can prevent it from destroying my life and the lives of our children. You have left me no choice but to separate from you. Therefore, I have filed a petition for divorce with the court and will follow through with divorce unless you give me a good reason to do otherwise. And I genuinely hope that you do.

*Today, I am presenting you two legal documents and you are free to choose either. One is a divorce decree; the other is a separation agreement. If you choose the divorce decree, you are admitting that you would rather continue to abuse alcohol than save our marriage. I will accept your decision, but I sincerely hope you will choose the separation agreement instead.*

*If you choose the separation agreement, we will remain married, but we will live apart. During this separation, I will remain faithful as your husband while you do whatever you must to live without alcohol and remain sober forever. You have destroyed any reason to trust your promises, so I must see a solid track record of healing and sobriety before I will feel confident living as husband and wife again. I long for that day and hope that you will make it possible.*

*I love you,*

*John*

The wayward spouse undoubtedly will experience shock, disbelief, denial, hurt, anger, or sorrow, and then he or she may try to bargain. None of these reactions demands a response. He or she should be allowed to vent without interference. Hopefully, any initial outburst will leave little fuel for retaliation or rancor later. And any decisions the wayward spouse makes on the spot should be accepted at face value but held loosely. They will likely change.

By the conclusion of the meeting, the wayward spouse must comprehend the following three points:

- The upright spouse wants the marriage to continue and remains committed to restoring the union, but he or she will no longer allow destructive behavior to impact the family.

- The wayward spouse has the power to decide the future of the marriage and may freely choose to either divorce or reconcile.

- Refusing to turn away from destructive behavior will lead to divorce, while repentance will lead to restoration.

Hopefully, acceptance will come in time, perhaps only after a long time; so effective communication must remain the primary objective. The meeting should be given as much time as needed to be certain the wayward spouse understands what has been communicated, and it should conclude soon thereafter.

After reading the letter, answering questions, and discussing the matter until the wayward spouse clearly understands what is happening, the divorce papers and the separation agreement, along with the confrontation letter, should be given to him or her. If some other method of delivery will satisfy the requirements of the court, this can be done as well, but the wayward spouse should not have to wait.

## Follow-Through

The confrontation marks the beginning of a new life for the upright spouse. However, this is not to suggest that the future will be easy. In fact, the first few days are likely to be difficult for a number of

We aren't declaring war; we're establishing boundaries.

reasons. First, everything will be different for the upright spouse and the children, which will require time for adjustment. Staying with family or friends for a short time will help ease the shock and reduce feelings of isolation. This would be the ideal time and place to explain everything to the children with as much detail as their ages permit.

The intense emotions experienced by the wayward spouse may lead to unwise, impulsive behavior. Preparation for the day of separation should anticipate the wayward spouse's probable actions, such as his or her likelihood of damaging property, seizing shared funds, or attempting to use the police or the legal system improperly. Each potential scenario should have a prearranged response.

The key word is *response*, not reaction or retaliation. We aren't declaring war; we're establishing boundaries. We aren't trying to dominate; we're trying to redeem. So, for example, if the wayward spouse has a history of demolishing valuables when upset, the upright spouse should secure them before the confrontation. If the wayward spouse is likely to change the locks on the home and place it on the market, a temporary order should be prepared—preferably ahead of time— and calmly presented at the right time. Each response must bring reasonable consequences, and the motivation must be to protect the interests and safety of the upright spouse, not to defeat his or her combative partner. Furthermore, communication from the upright spouse should be kept to a minimum and then conveyed with calm, rational love.

The state grants the wayward spouse, as the respondent, a given period of time in which to notify the court of his or her intentions regarding the petition. At this point, the responsibility for the future of the marriage rests in his or her hands. The upright spouse has only to respond to whatever decisions the wayward spouse makes. If the wayward spouse agrees to the separation but wishes to negotiate the specific terms of the agreement, then the upright spouse meets him or her at the bargaining table. If the wayward spouse prefers to end the marriage, then the upright spouse allows the divorce process to unfold like any other. If the wayward spouse turns combative and wants to drag the divorce through the courts, then the upright spouse must then fight hard for a fair settlement.

Once a good plan has been formulated and followed, and the wayward partner has been confronted with his or her sin and the offer of restoration, the upright partner has done all that can be done. Nothing more remains but to follow through on promises. Repentance finds redemption. Faithfulness earns trust. Consistency inspires restoration. And, if necessary, stubbornness reaps consequences.

Following through is straightforward enough. Doing what you say you're going to do isn't complicated, but it won't be easy.

## Seven

# From Gethsemane to Glory: A Personal Word to the Redeeming Spouse

Redemption is costly. For the redeemer more than anyone. God understands this. While He requires us to forgive the past, He does not demand that we expose ourselves to further injury. And let's face it; some relationships aren't worth the personal investment required to redeem them. Sometimes the sin is too great, the pain we must suffer to restore the relationship is too intense, and the fear we must overcome is too dreadful. Let me assure you that sometimes it's okay to walk away from a relationship. Restoration is entirely voluntary. However, what God *demands* and what God *desires* are two different matters. The former satisfies the requirements of the Old Covenant; the latter claims the blessings of the New Covenant.

When Adam and Eve sinned in the Garden, the Creator could have washed His holy hands of us and obliterated the entire universe right then and there. What He had created to be "good" became polluted with sin, through and through, and His holy character gave Him the right to execute justice. Yet He withheld His wrath and set aside His right to walk away from humankind. Moreover, this act of grace proved to be very costly. When He cursed creation—that is, revealed the consequences of sin—the triune God pronounced the greatest curse of all upon Himself. God would someday become a man in the person of Jesus Christ, a future "seed" of humankind, a God-man, who would be "crushed" by Satan (Gen. 3:15).

Two millennia ago, the Son of God came into the world the same way we did, except for one remarkable difference: a virgin suffered the agony of childbirth. He grew up in relative poverty in a despised little town in Galilee. He experienced all the joys and sorrows of existence in a fallen creation. Though entirely God, He was no less human than you or me and no less vulnerable to pain, infirmity, grief, and fear. Yes, even fear. Jesus knew that He had come to die for the sins of all humanity, to submit Himself to the unjust crushing of Satan on behalf of all people. And on the eve of His crushing, He flinched.

After breaking bread with His disciples and promising the comfort of the Holy Spirit to come, Jesus led them out into the night, across the Kidron Valley, and up the western slope of the Mount of Olives to a familiar retreat. He stationed His men at the entrance of a garden called Gethsemane and instructed them to pray, admitting, "My soul is extremely afflicted to the point of death" (Matt. 26:38).

Jesus was not a man given to overstatement. Mark used words that describe the kind of fearful astonishment that typically causes men to tremble[1] and then used a form of the Greek word *to fall* in such a way as to describe Jesus stumbling through the garden, praying, getting up, walking farther, falling again, and praying continually. Luke tells us, "His sweat became like drops of blood" (Luke 22:44). The dawn would commence an ordeal like nothing we can imagine, agony on a cosmic scale. All of sin's horrific affliction would become the unjust reward of Jesus' sinless obedience to the Father. And for what? You? Me? To restore His relationship with the very humanity that chose sin over intimacy with the Almighty?

Undoubtedly, the whispers of temptation clarified how absurd it was for the Son of God to suffer the penalty of sin. Nothing of God's righteousness demanded that He endure anything to redeem the worthless lot of disobedient humanity. In a garden at the beginning of time, God had a choice. He could exercise His holy right to banish all of creation from His presence or take our curse upon Himself for the sake of redeeming us. After thousands of generations of humanity added their own sins to Adam's, He stood again in a garden with the very same choice to make. Wash His holy hands of sinful humanity and return to the eternal, unspoiled intimacy of the Trinity, or . . .

In the frailty of human flesh, the Son of God pleaded with His Father, "If it is possible, let this cup pass from Me" (Matt. 26:39).

We know the end of the story. Jesus submitted. Not to the Law of the Old Covenant, which gave Him the right to walk away without suffering anything. No, He submitted to the will of the Father in order to establish a new law, the law of the New Covenant, the law of grace. The old Law said, *Do evil and you'll reap evil; do good and you'll reap good.* The new law of grace says, *Do as I do. Restore relationships with people who don't deserve your mercy. Trust My holy character, not only to preserve you through inevitable agony but to bring you immeasurable blessing as a result.*

You now stand in the center of your own Gethsemane.

Extending grace is an act of faith, especially when the grace comes at great cost to yourself.

Jesus was faithful; He submitted His own will to that of the Father. But wait, look again! Mark tells us He flinched a second time. And then again! After praying to be released from the law of grace and then submitting, saying, "Yet not as I will, but as You will" (Matt. 26:39), He emerged from the garden to find His disciples sleeping instead of praying. He admonished, "Keep watching and praying that you may not come into temptation; the spirit is willing, but the flesh is weak" (Mark 14:38). Then, "Again He went away and prayed, *saying the same words*" (Mark 14:39; emphasis added). According to Matthew, Jesus prayed for escape no fewer than three times.

At some point, after you have removed yourself from the chaotic, hostile, disorienting environment that was your marriage, your foggy state of mind will begin to clear. You will begin to see the pain you have endured with shocking clarity. Moreover, the power that comes from establishing and enforcing appropriate boundaries can be intoxicating. After the anger, after the sadness, and sometime shortly after acceptance, fear will set in. And the intensity of it can be astonishing. *What if my partner repents and accepts my offer of restoration?* The prospect of intimacy with the person who callously trampled your boundaries is almost unthinkable now that you have begun to experience normal life again.

You now stand in the center of your own Gethsemane.

## Responsible Grace

If you have suffered at the hands of a spouse who has abused or ignored the covenant of marriage, you have rights under the laws of the United States, and the intelligent use of our legal system can secure them for you. Furthermore, the command to forgive frees you from the past, but it does not demand that you submit to more destructive behavior. Restoration is a choice, not a mandate. God's invitation to submit to the law of grace is not a call to switch off your brain and throw yourself into the pit from which you just climbed.

If your mate has shown signs of repentance, take his or her gesture at face value, but only extend further trust when the trust you have previously given is honored with faithfulness. Genuine repentance does not merely promise to do better next time. Repentance is a state of brokenness accompanied by observable behavior—practical changes that go a long way toward rebuilding trust.

My good friend and former colleague at Insight for Living, Dr. Bryce Klabunde, has written a helpful article in which he describes six signs of genuine repentance. If these specific behaviors are not present in your wayward partner, you are wise to wait before taking another step toward restoration.

1. *Repentant people are willing to confess all their sins, not just the sins that got them into trouble.* A house isn't clean until you open every closet and sweep every corner. People who truly desire to be clean are completely honest about their lives. No more secrets.

2. *Repentant people face the pain that their sin caused others.* They invite the victims of their sin (anyone hurt by their actions) to express the intensity of emotions that they feel—anger, hurt, sorrow, and disappointment. Repentant people do not give excuses or shift blame. They made the choice to hurt others, and they must take full responsibility for their behavior.

3. *Repentant people ask forgiveness from those they hurt.* They realize that they can never completely "pay off" the debt they owe their victims. Repentant people don't pressure others to say, "I forgive

you." Forgiveness is a journey, and others need time to deal with the hurt before they can forgive. All that penitent people can do is admit their indebtedness and humbly request the undeserved gift of forgiveness.

4. *Repentant people remain accountable to a small group of mature Christians.* They gather a group of friends around themselves who hold them accountable to a plan for clean living. They invite the group to question them about their behaviors. And they follow the group's recommendations regarding how to avoid temptation.

5. *Repentant people accept their limitations.* They realize that the consequences of their sin (including the distrust) will last a long time, perhaps the rest of their lives. They understand that they may never enjoy the same freedom that other people enjoy. Sex offenders or child molesters, for example, should never be alone with children. Alcoholics must abstain from drinking. Adulterers must put strict limitations on their time with members of the opposite sex. That's the reality of their situation, and they willingly accept their boundaries.

6. *Repentant people are faithful to the daily tasks God has given them.* We serve a merciful God who delights in giving second chances. God offers repentant people a restored relationship with Him and a new plan for life. After healing comes *living*. Repentant people accept responsibility for past failures but do not drown themselves in guilt. They focus their attention on present responsibilities, which include accomplishing the daily tasks God has given them.[2]

Take some time to review the "Repentance Inventory" worksheet at the end of this book and reflect on your mate's behavior. Genuine repentance is very rare, but it is crucial to the success of restoration.

Without it, the rebuilt marriage will almost certainly crumble with even more devastating results.

## Observing the Law of Grace

If your partner appears to be authentically repentant, genuinely broken, then you have a difficult choice. Having completely forgiven your mate, you may exercise your right to keep a safe distance indefinitely. And if your mate has engaged in intimate physical contact of a sexual nature with another person, your union has been severed; you are free to walk away and never look back. Whether you have biblical grounds for a divorce or not, you are not bound by the Old Covenant to risk further harm at the hands of your mate. However, you must consider the law of grace.

What I am calling the law of grace is not like the system of rewards and punishments under the Old Covenant. It's really more of a principle, a law in the same sense that gravity is a law, a truth that operates whether we acknowledge it or not. And like the law of gravity, we can work against the law of grace, or we can allow it to work for us:

- The law of grace responds to brokenness with mercy.
- The law of grace places value on those who merit no worth.
- The law of grace sacrifices one's right to happiness and looks to the Father for joy.
- The law of grace trusts that imitating Christ allows us to share His glory.
- The law of grace is the foundational principle of what will become the new creation.

- The law of grace is a law God writes on one's heart (Jer. 31:31–34) so that it will beat in perfect rhythm with His.

When we submit to the law of grace and invest ourselves in the work of restoring a broken relationship, we can expect to receive several blessings.

## Closeness to God

Restoring a broken relationship requires faith, which always brings us closer to God.

Years ago, when I found myself paralyzed between two alternatives in a life-changing decision, a good friend asked a penetrating question. Given that neither choice was foolhardy, he asked, "Which option will require more faith?" I had no trouble answering. And I could not argue with his reasoning. He said, "Always choose the option that requires more faith. The Lord will honor even a misstep taken with complete dependence upon Him."

I can honestly say that every time I chose the more faith-stretching path, I grew stronger in my walk with God. These journeys have not always been easy or free from suffering, but I would not know the Lord nearly as well if I had always played it safe. And never has this been truer than when I chose to risk restoring a relationship with someone who had shattered my trust.

## Personal and Spiritual Growth

Restoring a broken relationship gives us the opportunity to experience personal and spiritual growth that might not otherwise be possible.

One person is rarely 100 percent responsible for the breakdown of a relationship. Our faults and failures will never excuse the sin of another; however, we often bear some responsibility. As repentance proves genuine and trust begins to rebuild, you will likely discover, as I have, that your own failures contributed to the sinful choice of the other person. If you walk away from this relationship, you will likely repeat the same pattern of behavior in another.

I have also discovered no greater means of knowing Jesus Christ personally than by imitating Him. When I became the conduit of grace in the life of another, I discovered more about forgiveness, acceptance, unconditional love, mercy, and kindness than a thousand sermons could have taught. As I gave to someone else what I had received from Christ and then personally experienced the immense cost of grace, I found myself increasingly grateful for the gift of salvation. Looking back on that experience today, I would not trade any of the pain and fear I suffered for the spiritual growth that I enjoy now.

## Build Closeness Without Complications

Restoring a broken relationship builds upon the strengths of the former closeness while leaving the complications behind.

Your mate certainly possesses some positive qualities, or you would not have been drawn to him or her in the first place. And you undoubtedly found joy and satisfaction in the relationship—at least in the beginning. Then, sometime later, issues began to develop and your partner chose behavior that essentially ended your marriage.

After your trust has been shattered, singleness might seem very appealing at first, but that's the pain talking. If you were not born with

> While God never wants sin to become the catalyst for intimacy, He will nonetheless use it—if we allow Him the opportunity.

what some call "the gift of singleness" (Matt. 19:12), the comfort of being alone will eventually grow old. If you need the intimacy of a mate, a fresh start with someone new can be an attractive possibility; yet all relationships must overcome personal challenges. Everyone has something unattractive that makes him or her difficult to live with. Only time will reveal what it is and how it will affect you.

Intimacy can only grow as the people in a relationship allow all of who they are to be seen and accepted by the other. And until all the ugliness is revealed, examined, addressed, and accepted, the relationship really hasn't begun. Too often people forfeit the chance to experience real intimacy because they nurture a fantasy that, out there somewhere, someone might be sinless enough to keep the spell of romance unbroken. So they allow disappointment to end one relationship only to begin another, which is also doomed to end in disappointment.

While God never wants sin to become the catalyst for intimacy, He will nonetheless use it—if we allow Him the opportunity.

## Embrace the Future

Restoring a broken relationship allows us to embrace the future with a clear conscience, no matter how it unfolds.

I wish I could promise that every dead or dying marriage could be revived and that every wayward spouse could be redeemed through redemptive divorce. Generally speaking, the longer the couple has enjoyed a good history in the marriage, the greater the chances of success. And, of course, the reverse is true. If the couple has not experienced very much good history, the wayward spouse will not be as motivated to recover the marriage. In his or her eyes, the loss is not all that great.

Across the board, the percentage of recovered marriages will be relatively low. I would consider one out of five an encouraging statistic. While I can't predict the future of the marriage, I can promise that following the redemption process through to conclusion will prepare you for a much brighter future. After shuffling off the sorrow of days past, you will step into a new life with no regrets, no second-guessing, no wondering, *What if I had done this instead of that?*

If your mate repents and you are able to restore your marriage, you will have a victory story to tell your grandchildren. But if your mate signs the divorce decree and walks away, you will be able to look any would-be critic in the eye and say, "I did everything possible to save my marriage, but in the end, my mate left me to pursue his or her sin." And believe me, you want to be able to say that, not only to your critics, but especially to that special someone you might someday meet.

## Gethsemane's Glory

As the sun rose on Gethsemane, Jesus stood victorious over temptation. A cohort of evil men then bound Him in chains, subjected Him to appalling humiliation and outrageous injustice, and condemned Him to a kind of death reserved for the worst of criminals. By noon that same day, on a blood-soaked plot of ground just outside the city walls, the Son of God suffered unspeakable misery to redeem any who would accept His sacrificial gift. And by sundown He was dead.

For any other man, that would be the end of the story. But this was no ordinary man. This was the Author of the New Covenant, the One to establish the law of grace. This new law states that death for the faithful is not something to be feared, but rather embraced as the means of receiving abundant new life. On the third day, Jesus rose from His tomb to reclaim the world from Satan, and He now sits in the throne room of heaven, where He receives the adoration of all creation. But this glory would not have been possible except for the grace that triumphed in Gethsemane.

The choice to pursue restoration with someone who caused so much pain will challenge your trust in God like no other trial. I will forever remember the anguish of my own Gethsemane, which lasted several weeks and finally brought me to the end of my own strength. The culminating crisis came one evening as I made my way to a class on the campus of Dallas Theological Seminary.

The papers had been in my wife's hands for several weeks as I awaited her decision. During that time, what began as a nagging worry grew into terrifying dread. If she repented and expressed a desire to reconcile, I would be honor-bound to work with her on restoring our relationship. I understood my "right" to walk away from the marriage, but I could not ignore the call of God to allow His grace to have its way in me. Furthermore, the focus of the course I was taking could not have been a coincidence. Fourth-semester Hebrew required a thoroughly researched translation and detailed study of the book of Ruth. For nearly five months we examined every word, pondered each literary device, and examined how the human author structured this ancient narrative to tell us something about God. The history of Ruth tells the story of how the Lord responded to a young widow's extraordinary grace with exceptional blessing.

God calls us to imitate His extraordinary grace, but He does not require it. The Lord doesn't pay us to empty our grace out on others; instead, He gives us greater access to everything that is His. This promise is unconditional, yet it requires that we release our hold on everything that feels secure and then cling to the goodness of God—and here's the hard part—by trusting that which we cannot see. That's *faith* in the Christian sense of the word. That's how we partake of the New Covenant. We become immersed in grace as we lavish unmerited favor on others, especially the least deserving. But let me warn you: abandoning oneself to grace feels like a leap from the Empire State Building.

One autumn evening, I walked toward the class building as night fell upon the campus. The enveloping darkness mirrored what I felt happening inside, and by the time I stepped off the elevator on the third floor, I knew I would not be able to attend class. I ducked into an empty room and sat quietly in the dark. I wanted to pray, but no words could express what I felt, so I silently laid my emotions bare like a wounded child pointing to his injury. The fear and sorrow shook my body as I cried for release. I begged Him for permission to simply put the past behind me, including my marriage, and to allow me to pursue a new life.

After nearly two hours, I sat emotionally spent, repeating the words over and over, "Your will, Your way, Lord. Give me the grace to obey." In Romans 8:28, the Lord promises to use every situation, every hardship for my ultimate benefit, even if it looks dangerous. I threw myself onto that promise. I anchored my desires to His unfailing goodness and to the certainty that He is right in all His ways. I accepted the truth that if He brought my wayward mate to repentance, it was to fashion a wonderful future for both of us. But I admit, my confidence stood on trembling legs. Although I emerged from my Gethsemane obedient, I would have to pray often for the courage to see the process all the way through to its conclusion.

Within a few weeks, the choice was made. The divorce decree was signed and accepted by the court.

Though the offer of grace was refused, God never fails to honor our submission to the law of grace. The outcome is not nearly as important as our obedience, for He calls us to be faithful, not successful. In time, my wounds healed, and I emerged from the difficult recovery process a whole man. I cared for my children, I trudged through the necessary details of life, and I allowed my life to lie fallow. At times, I tried to fill the emptiness apart from His provision, only to feel emptier when my coping failed to satisfy. And, in His time, joy returned, along with exceptional blessing.

If I learned nothing else, it's that grace begets grace. When the time was right—and much sooner than I expected—the Lord intricately wove events together to give me a joyful future and an extraordinary mate to share it with. He gave me Charissa. And I don't consider it any coincidence that her name is based on the Greek word *charis*, which means "grace."

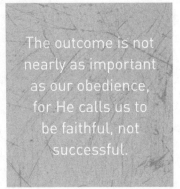

The outcome is not nearly as important as our obedience, for He calls us to be faithful, not successful.

I tell you my story, not because I did everything right. I didn't. By His strength and with the encouragement of godly people in my life, I submitted to the call of grace. And now I enjoy the benefits of obedience. I don't think my union with my wife would be nearly as strong if a long string of regrets and what-ifs had clung to me. Because I did everything humanly possible to restore my marriage with dignity, I can face the future without ever looking back. This is not only good for me; it's a gift of inestimable value to my mate. She knows my commitment to her will be no less complete, even in the face of failure.

I cannot predict your particular future, but I can guarantee that you will enter your own Gethsemane sooner or later. You will be tempted to withdraw the offer of redemption and protect yourself from further anguish. Let me encourage you to stay the course. Keep your boundaries firmly in place. Extend trust only as your partner proves faithful. And remain open to the possibility that the Lord may lead him or her through the long process of genuine repentance and complete transformation. In any event, stay the course.

Feel free to take as much time as you need to feel safe. You deserve patience, and your wayward spouse owes you nothing less. And trust the Lord. He is right in all His ways.

# Eight

## The Dangers of Grace

*Looking back, I know that I was not the only one in our home crying out to God. My precious husband was being broken; limb by limb he was dying to self. As he began to see the effects of his sins, he was undone. How is it that something so enticing one day becomes so hideous and vile the next. Oh, the power of sin, the danger that lies in taking our eyes off Christ! To see it retrospectively is both enlightening and frightening.*

*When James read his letter to me, I was moved by the sincerity and depth of his repentance. He had been focusing on Psalm 51, and his heart was indeed "broken and contrite." His actions were correlating with his words, and I couldn't hold back the forgiveness he deserved. I moved across the room to hug him, and he was overwhelmed. He later stated that while he knew both the Lord and I had forgiven him, it wasn't until I physically touched him again that he began to actually feel the cleansing take place.*

*Having gone through one of the most difficult stages of my entire life, I can boldly share 2 Corinthians 7:10: "Godly sorrow brings repentance that leads to salvation and leaves no regret, but worldly sorrow brings death" (NIV). Worldly sorrow is remorse without repentance. Godly sorrow brings forth repentance and the openness to allow that which was intended for evil to be used for good by God, ultimately leading to no regrets.*

*Mary Ann*

In 1888, Alfred Bernhard Nobel experienced something few ever will. He read of his own death in the headlines of a French newspaper. It was, of course, an error. The reporters had confused him for his brother, Ludvig, who had died while staying in Cannes. And, as if the mistake weren't distressing enough, the epitaph undoubtedly felt like a cold slap in the face:

THE MERCHANT OF DEATH IS DEAD.

Before Nobel's most famous invention, dynamite, excavators used nitroglycerin to blast holes through mountains and precious metals out of the ground. And the notoriously unstable chemical cost many men their lives. But dynamite changed everything. The explosive could be manufactured, transported, and handled safely, which allowed factory workers and construction laborers to do their jobs without wondering if each day would be their last. Unfortunately, the invention also brought upon humankind a great evil. The new compound could be used to blow up men as easily as rock or dirt.

Today we have the Nobel Prizes because an ill-timed epitaph taught the developer of modern explosives an important truth. Scientific revolutions, for all their wondrous possibilities, also allow evil men to multiply their evil. This principle also weighed heavily on Albert Einstein, the winner of the Nobel Prize for Physics in 1921.

Redemptive divorce is certainly no scientific revolution, nor is it a great philosophical leap. But, like any change for the better, this new way of thinking opens the door for several potential dangers.

## The Danger of Violence

*Redemptive divorce is not a remedy for domestic violence.* Redemptive divorce is intended to confront behavior that is destructive to the marriage, the household, and the people involved, including the wayward spouse. But marriages torn apart by physical abuse require a very different approach. Batterers are nearly always expert controllers, and trying to outwit them can become a dangerous prospect. Furthermore, abusive people desperately need control, and they are most volatile when con-

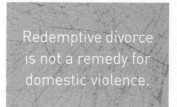

Redemptive divorce is not a remedy for domestic violence.

trol is taken away. Therefore, the redemptive divorce process, because it helps the upright partner reclaim power, will likely make matters worse, not better in these situations.

A nonabusive spouse who tenaciously clings to sin will likely respond negatively to confrontation and may even work aggressively—both in court and out—to keep things as they are. This is to be expected. However, if violence is probable, redemptive divorce is not the right approach. For information regarding this very complex marital issue and how to prepare for the unique challenges involved, consult *Broken and Battered: A Way Out for the Abused Woman* by Muriel Canfield. This poignant, insightful, and practical book is the best resource for someone trapped by domestic violence.

## The Danger of Unclear Objectives

When one spouse spends years trying to get the other to end his or her pattern of destructive behavior, the two unwittingly become enmeshed in a contest for control. As the unrepentant spouse deftly counters each threat to his or her cherished sin, the upright spouse feels compelled to try and try again. The game actually creates an elaborate system of denial that serves the needs of both partners. One spouse retains exclusive right to the title "Defender of the

Marriage," while the other gets to avoid taking responsibility for anything. Unfortunately, redemptive divorce can become yet another attempt to maneuver the wayward partner into doing what is right. And so the contest for control continues.

In crafting the two documents, a well-meaning attorney might try to use one as a carrot and the other as a stick. Fortunately, no-fault standards in many states make this difficult to do. I say *fortunately* because genuine redemption can never be coerced. Forced apologies don't heal relationships. A choice for reconciliation made under duress merely creates the illusion of unity. The marriage-destroying sin will simply go underground, only to resurface later with even more tragic results.

> The objective of redemptive divorce is to establish healthy boundaries for the upright spouse without robbing the offending spouse of his or her dignity as a moral agent accountable to God.

The objective of redemptive divorce is to establish healthy boundaries for the upright spouse without robbing the offending spouse of his or her dignity as a moral agent accountable to God. This can be done only by reducing the decision to a simple choice between continued marriage and continued sin. Therefore, all other motivations for choosing right or wrong must be removed from the equation.

## The Danger of Impure Motives

Divorce attorneys typically measure success by the size of the settlement they win for their clients, usually because their clients retain them to do just that. Redemptive divorce, on the other hand, must be fueled by a spirit of selfless love for the unrepentant spouse. We must be shrewd and discreet, but only to benefit the wayward partner, not to win big in court for the sake of selfish gain. If we subdue the unrepentant spouse, it must be to free a dearly loved partner from the trap of sin and to restore him or her to a place of honor.

Unfortunately, redemptive divorce can begin well and then turn ugly before it's over. When the upright spouse begins to experience a normal life free from the chaos created by his or her sinning partner, when he or she feels the first rush of empowerment after establishing boundaries, anger can take over. And this initial taste of freedom and power can be intoxicating.

Many will not emerge from their Gethsemane submitted to the law of grace. These children of the New Covenant will exchange unseen future blessings for their rights under the Old Covenant. Redemptive divorce, like the Christian life, must end well before we can call it a success. And many will count it a failure because they refused to be guided by love.

Grace is costly. It demands we pay a price for the love that we give the unworthy, beginning with our right to fair treatment. But it's the only way to partake of Christ's glory in God's economy and the only true measure of success in redemptive divorce.

## The Danger of Criticism

People suffering in dysfunctional marriages live in a murky world of confusion and misconception. Their common sense tells them one thing while the people they trust tell them the opposite. And these longsuffering guardians of their marriages never quite feel they can trust their own instincts. They live in a bifurcated world, one in which a thin veneer separates those who demand to know that everything is okay from those who are outraged by the reality that nothing is right.

The upright spouse must recognize that redemptive divorce means leaving this old world behind for one in which appearances and reality live in harmony. Unfortunately, this also means leaving many cherished relationships behind. A precious few from each side of the old world will accompany the upright spouse into this new existence, but many well-meaning family and friends will not. They simply cannot for several reasons.

First, they haven't read this book and only know divorce under the old paradigm. Divorce, in their minds, cannot have anything but an evil purpose. They view divorce as the unfaithful action of one partner rejecting the other. Divorce abandons and profanes the very institution of marriage. To divorce is to give up on the marriage and to suggest that God cannot mend the relationship if the two would just stick it out.

Second, they cling to a charming idealism that keeps them insulated from the ugly realities of a dysfunctional marriage. They don't experience the horrid visions of infidelity when they close their eyes, the anguish of wondering how the bills will be paid because the family income has been gambled away, the heartbreak of seeing the children's fingernails bitten down to the skin because someone might fly into a rage at any moment, the rancid odor of booze and vomit perpetually emanating from the bathroom, or the debilitating fear that the odometer might not fully account for what was done or who was seen on a particular day.

Third, because they have not experienced grace and do not live according to grace, they are not able to recognize grace when they see it. Like trying to explain the color red to someone born blind, no amount of explanation will ever allow them to understand the purpose of redemptive divorce.

Some legalists will take this even further. They give lip service to the grace of God but really care more about jots and tittles than people. They acknowledge the suffering but quickly condemn any choice but passivity and have no alternatives to suggest. These will not see the intentional grace of redemptive divorce because they refuse to see.

Fourth, when someone establishes and begins to defend healthy boundaries, his or her loved ones fear that the person they knew has been replaced by someone different. And in many respects, their fear has been realized. Indeed, a different person is emerging. Because people generally resist change, especially when it comes to relationships, they will likely feel betrayed and may even give support to the unrepentant spouse.

The next several years will be marked by misunderstanding, false accusations, attempts to coerce or control, and outright rejection. When Jesus took a bold stand for truth, He had to stand alone. His relationship with the Father and the indwelling of the Holy Spirit sustained Him. The upright spouse, if he or she remains faithful to the process, will discover a reservoir of inner strength never before tapped and will know by experience that the Lord is indeed enough. That in itself is worth risking the step of faith this process requires.

## The Danger of Misuse

Some will undoubtedly pursue divorce for selfish reasons, give it a pretty wrapping, and call it redemptive. Some tragically codependent partners, people who are deeply insecure or lacking self-respect, will also find in redemptive divorce yet another means of keeping the game of emotional cat and mouse going. Still others will apply the process to any behavior they find unpleasant or use redemptive divorce as a means of maintaining control in the marriage. Unfortunately, any attempt to define which situations warrant the drastic measures I have described in this book quickly leads to petty quibbling and futile hairsplitting.

Redemptive divorce is an expression of grace to the wayward spouse and a means of grace for his or her suffering partner. Only the upright spouse knows when enough is enough and at what point nothing else will save the marriage. He or she must eventually stand before God to give answer for his or her actions. So in any given situation, each of us will have to determine for ourselves whether we can support someone pursuing this very strong course of action.

Let's face it; grace is dangerous. It leaves the door wide open for people to turn it into a license for sin. When commenting on Paul's rhetorical question, "What shall we say then? Are we to continue in sin so that grace may increase?" (Rom. 6:1), David Martyn Lloyd-Jones wrote:

> The true preaching of the gospel of salvation by grace alone always leads to the possibility of this charge being brought against it. There is no better test as to whether a man is really preaching the New Testament gospel of salvation than this, that some people might misunderstand it and misinterpret it to mean that it really amounts to this, that because you are saved by grace alone it does not matter at all what you do; you can go on sinning as much as you like because it will redound all the more to the glory of grace. That is a very good test of gospel preaching. If my preaching and presentation of the gospel of salvation does not expose it to that misunderstanding, then it is not the gospel.[2]

The misuse and abuse of grace is not new. People always have and always will look for an opportunity to twist grace into something grotesque. Nevertheless, the abuse of grace doesn't diminish its beauty or make it any less amazing.

## The Upside of Redemptive Divorce

For all its inherent dangers and for all the hardships the upright spouse will likely face, this grace-filled, tough-love approach to unrepentant sin is a step in the right direction—for those suffering in dysfunctional marriages, for those who love them, and for all of us in the body of Christ.

### Redemptive Divorce Places Responsibility Where It Belongs

For some reason, we presently have dysfunctional marriages turned upside down. We look to the upright partner to hold the marriage together when it is the destructive behavior of the wayward partner that has placed it in jeopardy. We wag our heads at the unrepentant spouse, but we wag a finger at his or her longsuffering partner with the warning, "Whatever you do, don't divorce!"

Redemptive divorce places the burden of responsibility on the shoulders of the person guilty of destroying the marriage and holds him or her accountable to do what is right. And what a relief to the upright spouse! What an encouragement! If he or she only could feel that affirmation from family, friends, and church leaders.

### Redemptive Divorce Brings Truth out of the Shadows and into the Public Record

Men and women who nurture a love affair with sin frequently convince others, including their upright partners, that the fault lies somewhere else. They successfully fool a watching public and then play the role of the victim to perfection when their suffering mates eventually reach a breaking point and lash out through divorce.

Redemptive divorce gets the truth out on the table, which the court then validates, leaving no room for dispute. The wayward spouse must publically declare his or her choice between continued sin and restoration of the marriage. Should he or she choose divorce, the upright spouse has legal proof that every reasonable effort was made to keep the marriage together.

## Redemptive Divorce Leaves the Wayward Spouse Without Excuse and the Upright Spouse Above Reproach

Make no mistake, redemptive divorce is an ultimatum. Reasonable. Loving. Grace-filled. But an ultimatum nonetheless. It pares the failure of the marriage down to its essence: *You can have me or your sin but not both. Choose now.* If the sinning spouse winds up single with half the possessions he or she once enjoyed, who's to blame?

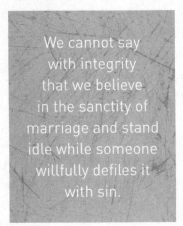

We cannot say with integrity that we believe in the sanctity of marriage and stand idle while someone willfully defiles it with sin.

Who can justly criticize the upright spouse? What should he or she do if the wayward spouse declares before the court, "I refuse to stop the behavior that victimizes my spouse and destroys my marriage!"? Go home and pretend like nothing happened? Who is *anyone* to suggest that a child of God should volunteer to be treated so disgracefully?

## Redemptive Divorce Honors the Institution of Marriage

In Reno, Nevada, a veteran noticed an American flag flying beneath that of another nation. He did not ignore the violation of American law or the affront to the institution it represented. He hauled the United States flag down, cut it loose with his Army knife, and then very likely gave it a dignified burial in accordance with the law. He did this in honor of the nation for which the flag stands.

We cannot say with integrity that we believe in the sanctity of marriage and stand idle while someone willfully defiles it with sin. And if we fail to hold the guilty partner accountable, we become his or her accomplice. Redemptive divorce, on the other hand, does not ignore an affront to the institution the Lord ordained. It honors the mystical union as sacred. It refuses to pretend everything is fine when, obviously, the union has been severed by destructive behavior.

## Redemptive Divorce May Be the Last, Best Catalyst for Restoration of the Marriage

Perhaps the most compelling argument for redemptive divorce is the hope it offers marriages destined for divorce court. Redemptive divorce is not the right remedy for sick marriages. It's intended for terminally ill marriages. Redemptive divorce is like a bone marrow transplant, an all-or-nothing procedure to be used only after every other treatment has failed.

When everything else has failed—counseling, interventions, rehabilitation, second chances, seventy-seventh chances—redemptive divorce just might provide the moment of clarity the wayward spouse needs. Perhaps the forced crisis will bring his or her destiny into clear focus right away and prompt a decision before regret closes the door behind him or her. The odds for success are admittedly low, but they are far better than the alternative: zero!

## A Word of Encouragement for the Redeeming Spouse

Very few people understood the mission of Jesus Christ on earth, including His own disciples. Many months into His ministry, perhaps even near the end, Peter boldly proclaimed, "You are the Christ, the Son of the living God" (Matt. 16:16), only to rebuke Jesus for predicting His own sacrificial death. "God forbid it, Lord! This shall never happen to You!" (Matt. 16:22). The disciples undoubtedly scratched their heads after watching Jesus cleanse the temple of the corrupt merchants and severely rebuke the religious leaders with eight woes, only to shed tears of compassion for them a few days later. His tough-love confrontation with the holy city must have been very confusing to others.

You can rest assured, many will not understand what you have chosen to do. To those who have not experienced your suffering, tough love appears unjust or, at least, unnecessarily harsh. They will have a difficult time seeing past the legal documents to see the love that motivates you. They cannot possibly appreciate the risk you take by extending grace to the person who has caused you and your children immeasurable harm.

Rest assured, God understands. You are not alone. You have partnered with Him in a great enterprise to redeem the world, beginning with your wayward spouse.

Therefore, having been justified by faith, we have peace with God through our Lord Jesus Christ, through whom also we have obtained our introduction by faith into this grace in which we stand; and we exult in hope of the glory of God. And not only this, but we also exult in our tribulations, knowing that tribulation brings about perseverance; and perseverance, proven character; and proven character, hope; and hope does not disappoint, because the love of God has been poured out within our hearts through the Holy Spirit who was given to us.

For while we were still helpless, at the right time Christ died for the ungodly. —Romans 5:1–6

As the voices of doubt ring in your conscience, as you inevitably begin second-guessing your decisions, remember this: the unrepentant sin of your spouse has invalidated his or her right to remain the object of your devotion; nevertheless, you have chosen to imitate Christ. And all you have requested in return is a response.

You have chosen to give to another what you have received from God. Unmerited favor. The offer of restored intimacy. Redemption. Grace.

No wonder most will not understand!

God bless you, faithful partner in marriage. You do well.

# Appendix I

## Repentance Inventory

Sometimes people merely pretend to repent in order to avoid loss or to retain control. And they can appear authentically sorrowful, only to return to their destructive behavior later. An obvious change in attitude and behavior always accompanies repentance. Have you observed the six signs of genuine repentance in your partner?

*1. Repentant people are willing to confess all their sins, not just the sins that got them into trouble.* Has your spouse demonstrated a desire to be completely honest about his or her behavior? Describe the response you would hope to see from your spouse.

*2. Repentant people face the pain their sin has caused others.* Has your spouse allowed you to express the intensity of emotions you feel — anger, hurt, sorrow, and disappointment — without trying to justify, minimize, or shift blame? Describe how your spouse reacts to your emotions.

*3. Repentant people ask forgiveness from those they hurt.* Has your spouse asked your forgiveness? Do you believe his or her sorrow is genuine? Does your spouse pressure you to say, "I forgive you"? Does he or she expect you to "get over it" without sufficient time to heal? Describe the attitude you hope to see in your spouse concerning his or her destructive behavior.

4. *Repentant people remain accountable to a small group of mature Christians.* What has your spouse done to address any issues that may have contributed to his or her destructive choices? What is your partner doing to avoid a relapse and to grow stronger as a God-honoring person?

5. *Repentant people accept their limitations.* Does your spouse resent your need for reassurance? Does he or she seem to understand the need for the rebuilding of trust over time? How does your partner respond to your request that he or she observe certain restrictions?

6. *Repentant people are faithful to the daily tasks God has given them.* Is your spouse putting forth good effort to fulfill his or her duties at work and at home? Is your partner moving forward in life with humility, or do you sense that he or she merely wants to get things back to normal as quickly as possible?

# Appendix 2

## Preparing to Live Apart

*While being reviled, He did not revile in return; while suffering, He uttered no threats, but kept entrusting Himself to Him who judges righteously.*
—*1 Peter 2:23*

**Shelter:** Describe what living arrangement would best suit you and your children for the next several weeks. Be as specific as you can.

_____

_____

Where do you think you could live if your spouse refuses to move out?

_____

_____

**Security:** Describe the financial arrangements you would most favor during separation. This should include provision for living expenses, continued health care, protection of your credit rating, and so on.

_____

_____

What is the most likely means of financial support for you and your children during separation should the court *not* award temporary support?

_____

_____

**Stability:** Describe how the new living and financial arrangements would provide greater *practical* stability for the children and yourself than continued cohabitation.

_____

_____

How have your children and you suffered physically as a result of your spouse's destructive behavior?

_____

_____

**Sanity:** Describe how the new living and financial arrangements would provide greater *emotional* stability for the children and yourself than continued cohabitation.

_____

_____

What testimony or official records demonstrate how your children or you have been negatively impacted by your spouse's destructive behavior?

_____

_____

# Appendix 3

## Monthly Household Expenses

| Fixed Monthly Expenses | |
|---|---|
| Mortgage or rent | |
| Homeowners' association dues | |
| Childcare | |
| Health insurance | |
| Auto insurance | |
| Other insurance | |
| Auto loan payments | |
| Credit card payments | |
| Other loan payments | |
| | |
| **Variable Monthly Expenses** | |
| Groceries | |
| Utilities | |
| Telephone | |
| Electric/Gas | |

| Variable Monthly Expenses | |
|---|---|
| Cable/Internet | |
| Water/Sewer/Garbage | |
| Gasoline | |
| Clothing | |
| Medical/Dental (out-of-pocket) | |
| Healthy activities for the children | |
| Miscellaneous (attach examples) | |
| | |
| **Other Expenses** (per year, divided by 12) | |
| Education (tuition, fees, books, etc.) | |
| Taxes | |
| Auto repair/maintenance | |
| Home repair/maintenance | |
| Home insurance | |
| | |
| **Total Monthly Expenses** | |

# Appendix 4

## Documents Checklist

### Legal Documents

- ☐ Marriage license
- ☐ Prenuptial or postnuptial agreements
- ☐ Birth certificates or adoption documents for each child for whom you or your spouse are responsible
- ☐ Social Security numbers for each member of the household
- ☐ Divorce decree from former marriage

### Financial Documents

- ☐ Account statements for bank accounts, loans, IRAs, stocks, bonds, mutual funds, and other investments
- ☐ The most recent salary check stubs
- ☐ Tax returns for the past five years
- ☐ The most recent real estate tax bills
- ☐ Life insurance policies

- ☐ Loan documents either of you have signed
- ☐ Wills, living trusts, and other estate-planning documents
- ☐ Credit report from Equifax, Experian, and TransUnion for you and your spouse

# Appendix 5

## Preparing to Respond

*If your brother sins, go and show him his fault in private; if he listens to you, you have won your brother. But if he does not listen to you, take one or two more with you, so that by the mouth of two or three witnesses every fact may be confirmed. If he refuses to listen to them, tell it to the church; and if he refuses to listen even to the church, let him be to you as a Gentile and a tax collector.*

—Matthew 18:15–17

What behavior on the part of your spouse has compromised your marriage?

_____

_____

Describe the change in your spouse's behavior that would demonstrate genuine repentance. Be specific.

_____

_____

What must he or she *stop* doing? What should he or she *start* doing?

_____

_____

If your spouse were to repent and then affirm his or her desire to restore your marriage, what can he or she do to regain your trust?

_____

_____

What program or organization might encourage your mate to remain faithful to the restoration process and provide you with reasonable assurance of progress?

_____

_____

What accountability are you going to remain in as you work through the process of this divorce?

_____

_____

# Appendix 6

## Priorities for Negotiating the Settlement

| Item | Nonnegotiable | Of great importance | Of little importance |
|---|---|---|---|
| **Language of the Divorce** | | | |
| Fault divorce | ✓ | | |
| Description of grounds | ✓ | | |
| **Custody or conservatorship of the children, including the following *exclusive* rights:** | | | |
| The right to establish the primary residence of the children within the current state | | | |
| The right to establish the primary residence of the children across state lines | | | |
| The right to consent to medical, surgical, and dental treatment involving invasive procedures | | | |

| Item | Nonnegotiable | Of great importance | Of little importance |
|---|---|---|---|
| The right to consent to psychiatric and psychological treatment | | | |
| The right to consent to travel across state lines and abroad | | | |
| The right to receive and give receipt for periodic payments for support and to manage these funds | | | |
| The right to represent the children in legal action and to make other substantial legal decisions | | | |
| The right to consent to marriage and to enlistment in the armed forces of the United States | | | |
| The right to make decisions concerning the children's education | | | |
| The right to the services and earnings of the children | | | |
| The right to manage the estates of the children | | | |
| **Residence of the Children** | | | |
| During the week: | | | |
| On weekends: | | | |
| On holidays: | | | |

| Item | Nonnegotiable | Of great importance | Of little importance |
|---|---|---|---|
| **Visitation with the Children** | | | |
| Unsupervised visits: | | | |
| Supervised visits (describe limitations): | | | |
| During the week: | | | |
| On weekends: | | | |
| On holidays: | | | |
| **Monetary Support** | | | |
| For the spouse | | | |
| For the children | | | |
| **Division of Assets** (List only nonnegotiable assets) | | | |
| | | | |
| | | | |
| | | | |
| | | | |
| **Division of Debt** (List only nonnegotiable debt) | | | |
| | | | |
| | | | |
| | | | |

# Suggested Resources

Alsdurf, James and Phyllis Alsdurf, *Battered into Submission* (Downers Grove: InterVarsity, 1989).

Canfield, Muriel, *Broken and Battered: A Way Out for the Abused Woman* (West Monroe, LA: Howard, 2000).

Carder, Dave, *Torn Asunder: Recovering from Extramarital Affairs*, rev. ed. (Chicago: Moody, 1995).

Cloud, Henry and John Townsend, *How to Have that Difficult Conversation You've Been Avoiding* (Grand Rapids: Zondervan, 2005).

Cloud, Henry and John Townsend, *Boundaries: When to Say Yes, When to Say No to Take Control of Your Life* (Grand Rapids: Zondervan, 1992).

Dobson, James C., *Love Must Be Tough: New Hope for Families in Crisis* (Dallas: Word, 1996).

Ventura, John and Mary Reed, *Divorce for Dummies*, 2nd ed. (Hoboken, NJ: Wiley, 2005).

# Notes

## Chapter 1: Suffering or Divorce? Finding a Way Out of the No-Win Scenario

1. James Dobson, *Love Must Be Tough: New Hope for Families in Crisis* (Dallas: Word, 1996), 153.
2. James and Phyllis Alsdurf, *Battered into Submission* (Downers Grove: InterVarsity, 1989), 158.
3. The Greek word translated "immorality" in the New American Standard Bible is *porneia*, from which we get our word *pornography*. The term refers to sexual sin.

## Chapter 2: "The Marriage Is Over!" What Does that Mean?

1. Biblical Studies Press, *The NET Bible Notes* (Dallas: Biblical Studies Press, 2003), Gen. 2:18, text note 22.
2. John MacArthur Jr., *The MacArthur Study Bible*, electronic ed. (Nashville: Word, 1997), Gen. 2:24.
3. K. A. Mathews, *The New American Commentary*, vol. 1A, Genesis 1–11:26, electronic ed., Logos Library System (Nashville: Broadman & Holman, 2001), 216.
4. Tom Constable, *Tom Constable's Expository Notes on the Bible* (Richardson, TX: Galaxie Software, 2003), Gen. 2:24.
5. *Mishnah*, Quiddushin 1.
6. Michael S. Berger, "Marriage, Sex, and Family in the Jewish Tradition: A Historical Overview," in *Marriage, Sex, and Family in Judaism*, Michael J. Broyde and Michael Ausubel, eds. (New York: Rowman & Littlefield, 2005), 4.
7. David Instone-Brewer, *Divorce and Remarriage in the Church: Biblical Solutions for Pastoral Realities* (Downers Grove, IL: InterVarsity, 2003), 139.

## Chapter 3: The Biblical Divorce

1. David Werner Amram, *The Jewish Law of Divorce According to Bible and Talmud* (New York: Sepher-Hermon, 1975), 22.
2. David Instone-Brewer, *Divorce and Remarriage in the Church: Biblical Solutions for Pastoral Realities* (Downers Grove, IL: InterVarsity, 2003), 55.
3. A notable parallel would perhaps be the issue of flag burning. Many good Americans would defend a person's right to burn the American flag in protest, but personally despise the act as well as the person doing it.
4. Jesus most likely intended this in the figurative sense, referring to Himself and others, including perhaps John the Baptizer.
5. Whether or not this includes viewing pornography is debatable as this is clearly a gray area between mental and physical sexual expression. It's more than mere lust, yet falls short of actual contact with someone else. Because this didn't exist in Jesus' day, we cannot say for certain whether viewing sexual images severs the marital bond in God's eyes.
6. Geoffrey W. Bromiley, *The International Standard Bible Encyclopedia, Revised*, vol. 1 (Grand Rapids: Eerdmans, 1988), 773.
7. Many even prohibited remarriage for those whose partners had died, which is clearly contrary to Paul's teaching.
8. Alexander Roberts, James Donaldson, and A. Cleveland Coxe, *The Ante-Nicene Fathers*, Vol. II: Fathers of the Second Century: Hermas, Tatian, Athenagoras, Theophilus, and Clement of Alexandria (Entire) (New York: The Christian Literature Company, 1896), 6.
9. Ibid., 21.
10. Alexander Roberts, James Donaldson, and A. Cleveland Coxe, *The Ante-Nicene Fathers*, Vol. I: The Apostolic Fathers with Justin Martyr and Irenaeus. (New York: The Christian Literature Company, 1896), 188.
11. Alexander Roberts, James Donaldson, and A. Cleveland Coxe, *The Ante-Nicene Fathers*, Vol. III: Latin Christianity: Its Founder, Tertullian (New York: The Christian Literature Company, 1896), 405.

## Chapter 4: When Love Has to Get Tough

1. James Dobson, *Love Must Be Tough: New Hope for Families in Crisis* (Dallas: Word, 1996), 19.
2. Henry Cloud and John Townsend, *Boundaries: When to Say Yes, When to Say No to Take Control of Your Life* (Grand Rapids: Zondervan, 1992), 31, 35.
3. Some suggest this refers to an ancient punishment whereby a public official subjects a prostitute to public shame by tearing her clothes off in front of witnesses. However, the evidence for this in Israel is scant.
4. Cloud and Townsend, *Boundaries*, 45–46.

## Chapter 5: Putting Divorce Proceedings into Perspective

1. This assumes the partner who moved out did so with the intent to abandon and remained away for one year or more.
2. John MacArthur Jr., *The MacArthur Study Bible*, electronic ed. (Nashville: Word, 1997), Matt. 18:17.
3. Neil T. Anderson, *The Bondage Breaker* (Eugene, OR: Harvest House, 1990), 195. Used by permission.
4. Henry Cloud and John Townsend, *How to Have that Difficult Conversation You've Been Avoiding* (Grand Rapids: Zondervan, 2005), 75.
5. Dave Carder with Duncan Jaenicke, *Torn Asunder: Recovering from Extramarital Affairs*, rev. ed. (Chicago: Moody, 1995).

## Chapter 7: From Gethsemane to Glory: A Personal Word to the Redeeming Spouse

1. Gerhard Kittel and Gerhard Friedrich, eds., *Theological Dictionary of the New Testament: Abridged in One Volume*, trans. Geoffrey W. Bromiley (Grand Rapids: Eerdmans, 1985), 312.
2. Bryce Klabunde, "'I'll Change, I Promise': Six Signs of Real Repentance," unpublished article originally used in the ministry of Insight for Living. Used by permission.

## Chapter 8: The Dangers of Grace

1. Muriel Canfield, *Broken and Battered: A Way Out for the Abused Woman* (West Monroe, LA: Howard, 2002).
2. David Martyn Lloyd-Jones, *Romans: An Exposition of Chapter 6, the New Man* (Grand Rapids: Zondervan, 1973), 8–9.

# About the Author

See also p. 30

Following a fifteen-year career as an engineer, Mark W. Gaither earned a master of theology degree from Dallas Theological Seminary where he discovered his love for teaching and writing. After writing for Dr. Frank Minirth, he served as the director of creative ministries and writer for *Insight for Living*, the radio ministry of Chuck Swindoll, during which time he also served as Dr. Swindoll's editor and research assistant, a role he continues to enjoy.

Mark and his wife, Charissa, reside in Frisco, Texas, and have four children—Lauren, Parker, Robert, and Heather—who attend college. In addition to writing, teaching, and speaking at events and churches around the country (individually and as a couple), Mark and Charissa lead single adults at Stonebriar Community Church.